Joe Simmer's Creole Slow Cookin'

J o e

CREATED BY

Michael Ledet & Richard Stewart

NEW ORLEANS
2006

Some of the information presented in this book may not be quite true, as Joe possesses a wild and fertile imagination. Any similarities to events, real or unreal, or persons living or dead, are probably coincidental.

All research for Joe Simmer's Creole Slow Cookin' has been done in fair usage.

JULY 6, 2006

2 MARTINI PRESS, LLC FIRST EDITIONS

Published in the United States by 2 Martini Press, LLC, New Orleans, Louisiana

ISBN 0-9787823-0-5

Printed in Canada by Friesens Book Division

5500 Prytania Street
#616
New Orleans, LA 70115
www.2martinipress.com

Acknowledgments

JOE WOULD LIKE TO GIVE THANKS to all those who helped make this book plausible.

Our illustrious illustrators, including Alcide "Al" Guidry, Etienne Simoneaux, Ozema "Bill" Fortier, John Washington Smith, José Rrodiquez y Ortiz, Britto, Woodward "Woody" Williams and Edward Sketchworth Murphy for contributing their artistic talents and general insightfulness.

Melvin Poché, Dewayne Emelle, José Zima, Bax von Zimmer, Tennessee Williams, Nadine, Mademoiselle, Boudreaux, Manny "Lil' Sausage" Mancuso, Big Manny Mancuso, Ronnie Ragosa, Jenearl Simoneaux, Aunt Margaret, Mel Simmer, Martin Luther King, Poncho Villa, Mayor C. Ray Nagin, God, Bienville, and Bunny Simmer for their assistance and/or inspiration in recipe development.

All of his ancestors, including, but not limited to Baron Josef von Zimmer, Max von Zimmer (a.k.a. Mick Simmer), Joseph Maxwell Simmer, Honey Poché, Martine deLesseps Simone, Jacque Latour Simoneaux, Josephine Poché Simoneaux, Giacomo Giuseppe Simoni, Lola Simone Latour, Jolie Simoneaux Poché, Simone "SiSi" Simmer, Anthony Joseph Simmer, Sr., Josephine "Lady Joe" Simmer and Anthony Joseph "Mr. Junior" Simmer, Jr. for making Joe possible.

For their kind thoughts and words, Saunter Landry, Steve Stevenson, A. J. Frey, Jil Parker-Goldberg, Fjnvk Knutsen, Jacque deMaurepas, Vander Essex and Fant Gender.

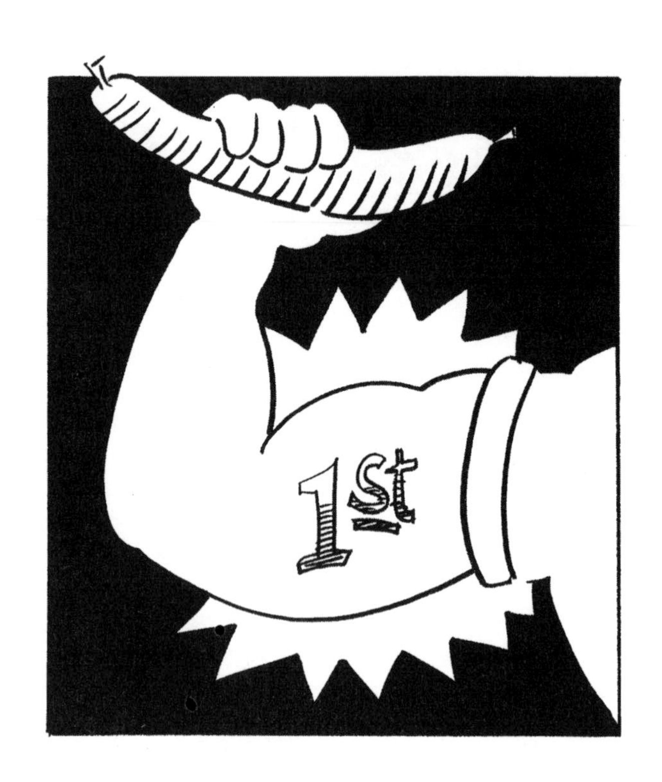
1st

Table of Contents

Many have tried to capture Joe, but Joe is Joe is Joe . . .

Foreword

AT FIRST IT MADE NO SENSE, and I was, to say the least, skeptical. Write a foreword for a slow cooker cookbook? A slow cooker cookbook with real recipes? With "gourmet" recipes? I did not think such a thing was possible. Then I heard two words that changed my whole perspective. Joe Simmer. The book's author is Joe Simmer. Say no more.

It was in the early 1990's when Joe Simmer burst upon the New Orleans culinary scene. As featured food and restaurant columnist for the venerable Offbeat magazine, he stirred things up in that food-focused town, and ruffled more than a few fine feathers. One thing led to another, and after closing his legendary restaurant and "talk of the town" catering business, he moved to New York City for a few years where he made a splash in the art world. He occasionally played a little music and dabbled in some local theater, while still pursuing his consulting business.

Joe enjoyed these creative outlets, yet felt a slow, steady, constant yearning to jump back into the food world. This time, though, not as a critic, and not back into the rough and tumble restaurant world. This time he felt something special and big brewing—something he would later term "the call of the crock."

Seeing the slow cooker craze coming, Joe knew he was the man to take it to the next level. All his education, all his life experiences led him to this point. And lucky for us, at this point he's in New Orleans.

What brought Joe home was what he calls "the four F's"—family, friends, food, and fun. New Orleans always had plenty of all that, but now that Joe's back we have even more!

It's been said that some people eat to live, while others live to eat. Now—thanks to Joe Simmer's Creole Slow Cookin', we can do both!

—SAUNTER LANDRY

What the critics are saying about Joe's art:

SIMMER'S WORK IS INFORMED BY PROCESS, by slow transformation of disparate organic elements melding into one—a symbiotic synthesis, if you will. To say that the whole is greater than the sum of its parts does not do no injustice to the whole or the parts, which by Joe's hand transcend their form and textural boundaries during their course of becoming; slowly—mythically, with no evaporation of meaning or substance.

—VANDER ESSEX
Art Critic
New York City

Introduction

FOOD HAS ALWAYS BEEN CENTRAL TO LIFE IN NEW ORLEANS, as has slowness, and perhaps it is because of that slowness that the two were not put together in book form earlier. What a natural combination!

New Orleans was founded in 1718, and slow cookers were invented in 1971. While it may be more than a coincidence that both events occurred in the past, their union in the present is a match made in heaven—"a heaven right here on earth"—as New Orleans has been called in song and story.

So many old time Creole favorites were simmered all day in cast iron pots over low, gentle flames. Red Beans and Rice, Greens, Gumbo, and Grillades are all naturals for the slow cooker. Here you will also find dishes of the various ethnic groups–French, Spanish, African, Italian, Irish and German—that make up the "cultural crock pot" that is New Orleans.

This book is divided into sections on soups and gumbos, beans—probably the perfect intersection of Creole cooking and slow cooking—entrees, including chicken, beef, pork and seafood and a lagniappe section of basic stocks. A special Post-Katrina section celebrates the enduring spirit, resiliency, and humor of New Orleans.

The remainder of this introduction will clue you in on the basics of Creole cooking—for those who have never made a roux—and some slow cooker basics for those new to the crock.

Creole Basics

The easiest way to get a handle on the characteristics of Creole food and its preparation is to read a few recipes, especially some of the gumbo and etouffée recipes. You will notice a commonality of methods and ingredients. Often a roux, usually a seasoning vegetable trio of onion, bell pepper, and celery, a main meat or seafood, and a coinciding stock.

MAKING A ROUX

Properly preparing a brown roux may be the step least familiar to the nascent

Creole cook. Essential to the flavor and color of many dishes, roux requires high heat and must be prepared in a pan on the stove before being added to the slow cooker. These instructions make it quick and easy.

Roux is essentially flour cooked in some sort of fat until it is evenly browned to the desired color. Most recipes call for either a dark roux, the color of chocolate (in the range between milk chocolate and bittersweet chocolate), or a medium roux, about the color of peanut butter.

Here's how you make it: Set a heavy-bottomed pan over a medium-high heat. The pan should be large enough to hold the fat and flour, plus the chopped seasoning (onion, bell pepper, celery). Heat the fat or oil in the pan and blend in the flour with a wire whisk, making sure it is free of lumps. Continue cooking and stir constantly. When the roux stops bubbling, in will begin browning rapidly. Keep stirring with the wire whisk and pay close attention. As soon as the desired color has been achieved, stir in the chopped seasoning vegetables and remove the pan from the heat. The addition of the room-temperature vegetables will immediately lower the temperature and halt the browning process. Proceed with the recipe as directed.

Two points of caution: If the roux looks or smells burned, throw it out and start over as a burned roux will ruin a dish. And be careful of splashes while stirring and adding vegetables—roux is very hot!

THE CREOLE PANTRY

Having some basic ingredients on hand prevents running to the grocery store for some last minute essential.

Here's your grocery list of New Orleans staples: Black pepper, white pepper, cayenne pepper, dried thyme, bay leaves, salt, filé powder, all purpose flour, vinegar, olive oil, butter, bacon, canned diced tomatoes, fresh parsley, onions, green onions, green bell peppers, celery, tomatoes and garlic, frozen chicken stock, beef stock and seafood stock (or good quality packaged broth), and white and red wine for cooking and drinking while cooking. Page 125 lists sources for hard-to-find products

One more point on Creole food. Many of these pot cooked dishes taste even better the next day and most freeze well.

Joe stirs his slow cooker ONLY AS DIRECTED.

Slow Cooker Basics

The concept and practice of slow cooking has been around for centuries. A crockery pot nestled in the embers of a cave dweller's fire and left overnight is primordial slow cooking. Modern man uses electricity.

Today's slow cookers consist of a base with concealed heating elements wrapping around the sides of a crockery insert. Food is cooked by indirect heat over a long period of time. The high setting on most slow cookers is about 300ºF, low about 180ºF, and "keep warm" about 140ºF. *Cooker temperatures may vary slightly, so cooking times for each recipe are close, but approximate.*

A FEW OTHER THINGS TO REMEMBER

Generally, the crock should be filled at least half way, but not much more than three-fourths, unless specified otherwise.

Do not put prepared ingredients in the crock and refrigerate over night and then cook in the morning—a chilled crock will take too long to heat.

Conversely, don't put a freshly cooked crock of food in the refrigerator to cool and store. The crock takes too long to cool down. Transfer the food to other containers for cooling and storing.

While cooking, resist the temptation to peek. The heat you lose can equal about 10–15 minutes of cooking time, and stirring is unnecessary unless specifically called for in the recipe.

Slow cookers do not brown. Beef and pork look and taste better if prebrowned in a pan on the stovetop, or in a very hot oven. Unless browned first, chicken skin is very unattractive when slow cooked. However, skinless looks and tastes fine. Convenient boneless, skinless chicken thighs are a slow cooker natural.

SELECTING YOUR SLOW COOKER

Joe's simple, one word philosophy on life also applies to slow cooking:

anitcomplexification.

The most versatile and convenient model he has found is a 6 or 6½ quart oval shaped, programmable unit, preferably in brushed stainless steel with a black crock insert. This size easily accommodates a pound of dried beans and is perfect for a pot of gumbo. The oval shape works well for roasts and chicken, and the combination of brushed stainless and black crockery looks smart in Joe's kitchen.

Considering convenience as one of the primary benefits of slow cooking, a programmable slow cooker just makes sense. If you are preparing a dish that should cook for 4 hours, but won't be back home for 6 hours, the cooker will automatically stop cooking and switch to the gentle heat of the "keep warm" setting.

All recipes in this book have been prepared and tested in a 6 quart, oval shaped slow cooker.

JOE
SAYS
GO
SLOW

Soups and Gumbos

SOUP IN NEW ORLEANS means more than just Gumbo. Oyster and Artichoke Soup, Bean Soups, Turtle Soup, and Vegetable Soups are all part of the local play list, and all work well with a slow cooker. Gumbos take a little more prep time up front, but the effort is well rewarded, and you don't have to hang around and watch the pot all day.

Be sure to check out the Lagniappe section (page 117) for stock recipes. Homemade stocks really enhance a soup or gumbo, but there are also several good packaged products on the market—be sure to look for the all-natural, low sodium varieties.

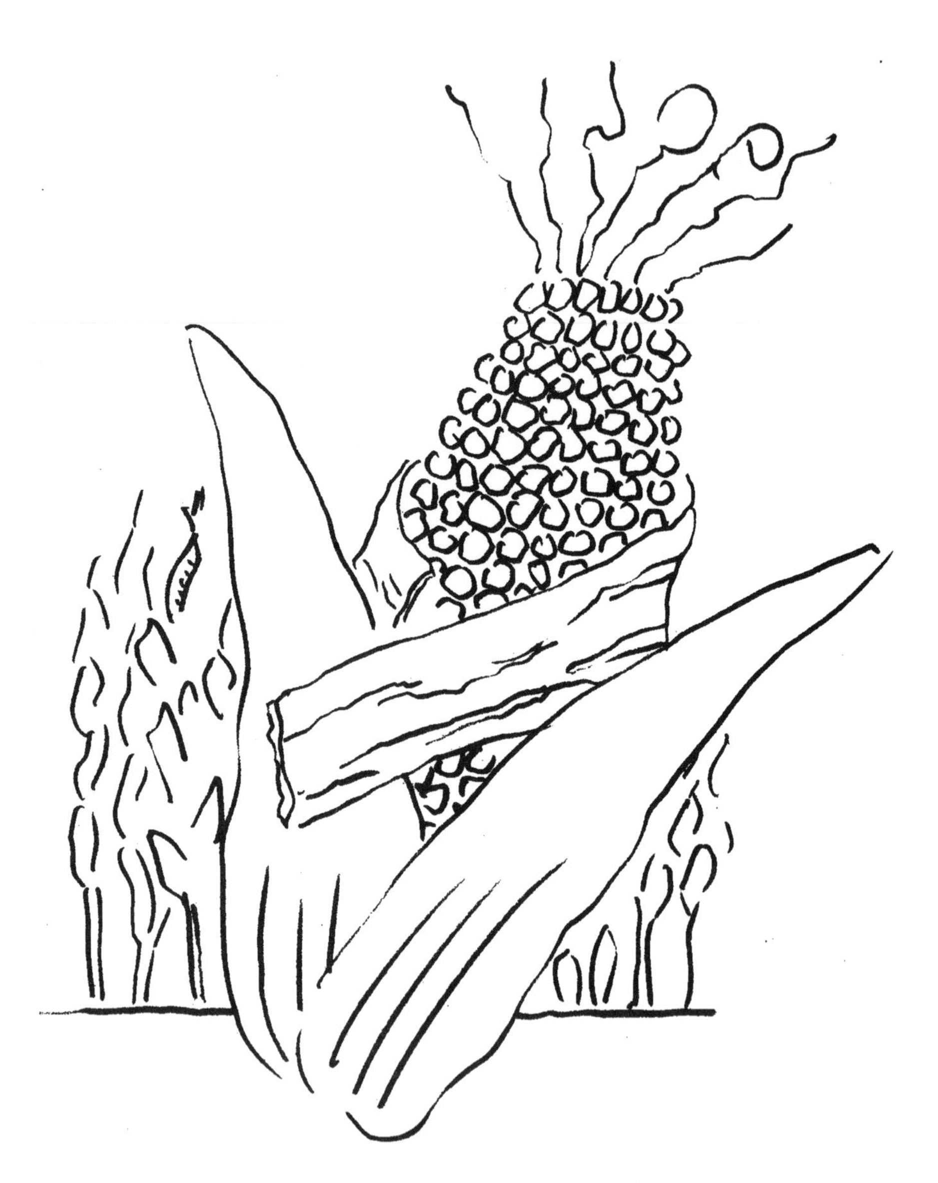

Joe's home-grown bacon wrapped corn.

Creole Corn Chowder

SERVES 8

- ¼ lb sliced bacon
- 1 cup chopped onion
- ½ cup chopped green bell pepper
- ½ cup chopped red bell pepper
- ½ cup chopped celery
- 1 teaspoon minced garlic
- ½ teaspoon black pepper
- 1 teaspoon white pepper
- ¼ teaspoon cayenne pepper
- 1 bay leaf, crushed
- ½ teaspoon dried thyme
- 1 teaspoon salt
- ¼ lb tasso, chopped
- 1½ cups chopped carrots
- ½ lb red potatoes, cut into ½ inch dice
- 1 lb corn kernels, fresh or frozen
- 2 14½ ounce cans creamed corn
- 2 cups chicken stock (page 119) or broth
- 1 cup heavy cream
- ½ cup finely chopped green onion

In a large skillet set over a medium heat, fry the bacon until crisp and set aside. Sauté the chopped onion, green bell pepper, red bell pepper, and celery in the bacon drippings for 10 minutes, stirring occasionally. Add the minced garlic, black pepper, white pepper, cayenne pepper, bay leaf, thyme, salt, and chopped tasso and cook for 1 minute. Transfer to the slow cooker and add the crumbled cooked bacon, diced carrots, diced potatoes, corn, creamed corn and chicken stock. Stir to mix, cover and cook on high for 3–3½ hours or low for 6–7 hours. If cooking on low, switch to high, add the heavy cream and chopped green onion and cook for 30 additional minutes.

Chef's Notes: *For a variation, and a more substantial dish, add 1 lb of peeled crawfish tails or cooked, diced chicken at the time you add the cream and green onions.*

WINE SUGGESTION: A crisp, dry, somewhat acidic white, such as a Sauvignon Blanc or Alsace Riesling. A cold beer would also be nice.

Chicken Andouille Gumbo

SERVES 8

ALWAYS ON HAND IN THE SIMMER HOUSEHOLD, sausage finds its way into many a slow cooked dish, and smoky, spicy Andouille sausage is one of Joe's favorites. This dish melds many of the myriad influences contributing to the "cultural crock pot" that makes Louisiana cuisine Louisiana cuisine.

- **½ cup olive oil**
- **½ cup flour**
- **2 cups chopped onion**
- **1 cup chopped bell pepper**
- **½ cup chopped celery**
- **2 cups diced tomato (or 1–14½ ounce can)**
- **¾ lb Andouille sausage, sliced**
- **1 lb frozen sliced okra**
- **3 bay leaves**
- **1 teaspoon dried thyme**
- **½ teaspoon black pepper**
- **½ teaspoon white pepper**
- **¼ teaspoon cayenne pepper**
- **1 teaspoon salt**
- **6 cups chicken stock (page 119) or broth**
- **1½ pounds boneless, skinless chicken thighs, cut into 1-inch pieces**

Set a heavy bottomed sauté pan over a medium-high heat. Add the oil and flour and cook, stirring almost constantly to make a medium brown roux. When the color is that of peanut butter or a little darker, add the chopped onion, bell pepper, and celery, stir well and turn off the heat. Transfer to the crock with all the other ingredients, stir to mix and cook on low for 6–7 hours.

Serve in large bowls with steamed rice.

WINE SUGGESTION: Almost anything red or a full-bodied white.

Joe's great-grandfather, Max von Zimmer, arrived in the U.S. as a very young child when his parents left the Rhineland and settled in the Bayou Lafourche-land of des Allemands, Louisiana. As a teenager, Max worked at the local butcher shop as a sausage stuffer, before moving to New Orleans in 1880. He settled in the neighborhood known as the Irish Channel, changed his name to Mick Simmer, and married Colleen Frye, whose father owned the neighborhood bar and po-boy shop. Mick and another new neighbor, A. J. Mancuso, soon opened their own sausage factory, the S&M Meat Works, specializing in Andouille, Italian sausage, and bratwurst. The next year, Colleen gave birth Joe's grandfather, Anthony Joseph Simmer.

Mick lived to the age of 106, and among Joe's earliest childhood memories is that of old Mr. Mick rocking rhythmically in his back porch chair, telling tales of ancient meat grinders and custom made stuffing machines.

Filé Gumbo

SERVES 6

- **1 chicken, skinned and cut into 8 pieces, about 3 lbs**
- **5 cups chicken stock (page 119) or broth**
- **2 cups chopped onion**
- **1 lb smoked sausage, sliced**
- **2 cups chopped celery**
- **2 cups chopped green bell peppers**
- **8 cloves garlic, chopped**
- **3 bay leaves, crushed**
- **2 teaspoons salt**
- **1 teaspoon black pepper**
- **¼ teaspoon cayenne pepper**
- **¼ cup filé powder**
- **¼ cup chopped green onion tops**

Place all ingredients except the green onion tops in the slow cooker and stir to mix. Cook on high for 5 hours or low for 9–10 hours. If possible, stir once or twice during the cooking process.

Serve in large bowls over steamed rice, and garnish with sliced green onion tops.

Chef's Notes: *As you can see, this gumbo contains neither roux nor okra. Filé, the dried, ground leaves of the sassafras tree serve as both a flavoring and thickening ingredient, and this gumbo is more Cajun than Creole in both origin and flavor.*

WINE SUGGESTION: An austere white Bordeaux or a lush red Côtes du Rhône, depending on your take on life.

Shrimp, Crab, and Okra Gumbo

SERVES 6–8

- **½ cup olive oil**
- **½ cup flour**
- **2 cups finely chopped onion**
- **1 cup finely chopped green bell pepper**
- **½ cup finely chopped celery**
- **1 lb peeled medium-sized shrimp**
- **8 ounces smoked sausage, diced**
- **1 lb frozen sliced okra**
- **2 cups chopped tomato, fresh or canned**
- **3 bay leaves, crushed**
- **¼ teaspoon allspice**
- **¼ teaspoon cloves**
- **1 teaspoon salt**
- **½ teaspoon black pepper**
- **¼ teaspoon cayenne pepper**
- **½ lb broken gumbo crabs**
- **3½ cups seafood stock or shrimp stock (page 122)**

Heat the oil in a large, heavy bottomed skillet set over a medium-high heat. Whisk in the flour and cook, stirring almost constantly, to make a dark brown roux. Remove the pan from the heat and add the chopped onion, bell pepper, and celery and stir to mix. Scrape the contents of the pan into the slow cooker along with all other ingredients. Cook on high for 5½ hours or low for 10–11 hours.

Serve in large bowls over steamed rice.

Chef's Notes: *This style of gumbo is enjoyed in restaurants and homes all over New Orleans. For a splurge, add a pound of lump or claw crabmeat 15 minutes before serving, allowing it to just heat through.*

WINE SUGGESTION: Something French from the Loire valley, an American Sauvignon Blanc, or a white Bordeaux

Gumbo Z'herbes

SERVES 8

"Z'HERBES" IS A BASTARDIZATION OF THE FRENCH "AUX HERBES", meaning "with herbs, or greens". This traditional New Orleans Lenten gumbo contains no meat, so it could be eaten on fast days, including Good Friday.

Joe once had a French girlfriend, Marie Claude, back in his late teens or early twenties. She was older than Joe, and a single mother with a six year old son named Beau, who used to call Joe "Jeaux." Joe's mother didn't approve of the relationship, but took some solace in that at least Marie Claude was Catholic.

½ cup olive oil
½ cup flour
2 cups chopped onion
½ cup chopped green bell pepper
½ cup chopped celery
2 tablespoons minced garlic
3 bay leaves, crushed
½ teaspoon dried thyme
½ teaspoon black pepper
½ teaspoon white pepper
¼ teaspoon cayenne pepper
2 teaspoons salt
2 quarts Roasted Vegetable Stock (page 121), or water, or a combination of the two
½ small head cabbage, cut into 1-inch squares
2 quarts cleaned, chopped collard greens
2 quarts cleaned, chopped turnip greens
1 bunch green onions, sliced
¼ cup chopped parsley
1 15 ounce can red kidney beans

Heat the olive oil in a large heavy-bottomed pot set over a medium-high heat. Whisk in the flour and cook, stirring frequently, to make a dark brown roux. Add the chopped onions, bell pepper, and celery, and cook, stirring occasionally for 5 minutes. Add the next 7 ingredients and cook for 1 minute. Stir in the vegetable stock and bring the pot to a boil, stirring occasionally.

Place the cabbage, collard greens, turnip greens, green onions, parsley, and red kidney beans in the slow cooker. Pour or ladle the roux/stock mixture into the crock, cover and cook on low for 3–3½ hours. After an hour or so of cooking, stir once to make sure all the cabbage, greens and beans are submerged in the liquid.

Serve in large bowls with steamed rice.

Early every morning, right after mass, Joe's aunt Margaret would head home to start work on the evening meal she prepared daily for her four grown sons. Ever since her husband left her she had dedicated her life to them. Three of the boys still lived at home, and the fourth would just come over for dinner, or have her drop it off at his apartment.

Aunt Margaret seemed to favor recipes involving lots of tedious scrubbing and chopping. An austere woman who rarely smiled, she savored self-sacrifice and knew the true virtue found in suffering. Her favorite dish was Gumbo Z'herbes. The extensive preparation always felt like a good penance, and she liked that she could cook it in May or December and pretend it was Lent. In fact, every day was Good Friday at Aunt Margaret's house.

Joe grows his own herbs.

Smoked Turkey and Hot Sausage Gumbo

SERVES 6–8

1 lb smoked turkey, thighs or legs
½ cup olive oil
½ cup flour
2 cups chopped onion
1 cup chopped green bell pepper
½ cup chopped celery
1 tablespoon filé powder
4 cups chicken broth or stock
1 cup water
1 lb smoked hot sausage, sliced
1 teaspoon salt
1 teaspoon dried thyme

Skin and bone the smoked turkey and cut the meat into 1-inch cubes. Set aside.

In a large, heavy bottomed saucepan, heat the olive oil over a medium-high heat, whisk in the flour and cook, stirring almost constantly, to make a peanut butter colored roux. Remove the pan from the heat and stir in the onion, bell pepper, and celery. Transfer the contents of the pan to the slow cooker, and add all remaining ingredients. Stir to mix, cover and cook on high for 4 hours or low for 7–8 hours.

Serve in large bowls or soup plates with steamed rice.

Chef's Notes: *If you use fresh (un-smoked) hot sausage, cook it first and drain on paper towels to avoid excess fat in the gumbo.*

WINE SUGGESTION: An Australian or California chardonnay or a nice Syrah. If you enjoy "off-dry" whites, a German Riesling or Gewurztraminer would work well with the smoke and spice.

Oyster and Artichoke Soup

SERVES 4–5

½ cup butter
1½ cup finely chopped onion
1 cup finely chopped celery
1 tablespoon minced garlic
¼ teaspoon ground nutmeg
½ teaspoon dried thyme
½ teaspoon black pepper
½ teaspoon white pepper
⅛ teaspoon cayenne pepper
1 teaspoon salt
⅓ cup flour
1½ cups chicken stock (page 119) or broth
1 14 ounce can artichoke hearts, drained, rinsed and coarsely chopped
1 cup heavy cream
1 pint shucked oysters, drained (about 2 dozen)
2 tablespoons chopped parsley

Melt the butter in a large heavy-bottomed saucepan set over a medium heat. Add the finely chopped onion, celery, and garlic and sauté, stirring occasionally, for about 10 minutes. Stir in the next 7 ingredients and cook 1 minute. Add the chicken stock and stir until evenly blended in. Transfer the contents of the pan to the slow cooker and stir in the chopped artichoke hearts and the heavy cream. Cover and cook on low for 3 hours.

Stir the soup well, scraping up and mixing in any bits stuck to the sides of the crock. Adjust the seasoning and add the drained oysters and the chopped parsley. Cover and cook 10 minutes, or until oysters are just curled around the edges.

Serve in large soup plates with lots of hot French bread.

WINE SUGGESTION: First choice—Muscadet, Pinot Grigio, or a dry Alsace Riesling. Second choice—Sauvignon Blanc or a white Graves

Duck Gumbo with Oysters

SERVES 6–8

2 small ducklings, about 5–6 lbs total
½ cup butter or bacon drippings
½ cup flour
2 cups chopped onion
2 cups chopped green bell pepper
1 cup chopped celery
1 tablespoon filé powder
1 bay leaf, crumbled
1 teaspoon black pepper
½ teaspoon white pepper
½ teaspoon cayenne pepper
1 teaspoon salt
1 14½ ounce petit cut diced tomatoes
4 cups chicken stock (page 119) or broth
1 pint shucked oysters, drained (about 2 dozen)

Roast the ducks according to the directions on the package, and drain off the rendered fat, or purchase four pre-roasted duck halves. Remove the skin from the ducks and cut each into 10 pieces—2 legs, 2 thighs, and each breast cut into 3 pieces. Place the duck pieces in the slow cooker.

Heat the butter or bacon drippings in a large, heavy bottomed pot set over a medium-high heat. Whisk in the flour and cook, stirring frequently to make a dark brown roux. As soon as the roux is the color of milk chocolate, add the chopped onion, bell pepper, and celery. Cook, stirring occasionally, for about 5 minutes. Stir in the next 7 ingredients and cook 1 minute. Add the tomatoes and chicken stock and stir to mix. Pour the mixture into the crock, cover and cook on low for 3½–4 hours.

Adjust the seasoning, add the drained oysters and continue cooking on low for 10–15 minutes, or until oysters are just curled around the edges.

Serve in large soup bowls over steamed rice.

Chef's Notes: *If you have a smoker, try smoking the ducks instead of roasting them. The smoky flavor works quite well with oysters.*

WINE SUGGESTION: If you are going with white, try a Viognier or fuller-bodied Chardonnay. If you prefer red, find a medium-bodied Pinot Noir or a nice Chianti.

Creole Vegetable Soup with Beef Brisket

SERVES 8–10

2 lbs beef brisket
1 teaspoon salt
½ teaspoon black pepper
½ teaspoon white pepper
¼ teaspoon cayenne pepper
1 tablespoon olive oil
2 cups chopped onion
1½ cups sliced celery, ¼-inch slices
1 tablespoon minced garlic
1 bay leaf, crushed
1 teaspoon dried thyme
½ cup chopped parsley
½ small cabbage, cut into 1-inch squares, about 4 cups
2 medium turnips, scrubbed and cut into ½-inch dice, about 2 cups
3 large carrots, sliced into ¼-inch slices, about 2 cups
1 14½ ounce can diced tomatoes
7 cups water
1 teaspoon salt, or to taste
¾ cup catsup
¼ cup prepared horseradish, or to taste

Trim the excess fat from the brisket and, if necessary, cut it into pieces that will fit into the slow cooker. Combine the salt, black pepper, white pepper, and cayenne pepper and season the meat, rubbing it into all surfaces. Heat the oil in a skillet. Set over a high heat and quickly brown the meat on all sides. Set aside.

Reduce the heat to medium-high and sauté the chopped onion, celery, and garlic for 5 minutes. Transfer to the crock along with the bay leaf, thyme, chopped parsley, chopped cabbage, diced turnips, sliced carrots, stewed tomatoes, and water. Stir to mix and set the browned brisket on top, pushing it down into the vegetables enough so that it does not touch the lid when covered. Cover and cook on high for 4 hours or low for 8 hours.

Remove the brisket and set aside to cool a bit. Add salt to the soup if necessary. Combine the catsup and horseradish to make cocktail sauce and set aside.

To serve in the traditional New Orleans manner, ladle the soup into large bowls. Slice the brisket and serve on side plates with the cocktail sauce.

Chef's Notes: *If you prefer, when the soup is done, cut the beef into serving-sized chunks, return it to the crock and serve it all in soup bowls, omitting the cocktail sauce.*

Red Bean and Ham Soup

SERVES 8–10

LIKE MANY A NEW ORLEANIAN, Joe holds a special place in his heart for Red Beans and Rice. But some Mondays he's just not in the mood for rice, and would really prefer a soup, perhaps cooked with a little wine for that gourmet touch. That's why he invented this delicious dish.

- **1 lb dried red kidney beans**
- **6 cups water**
- **2 cups chopped onion**
- **1 cup chopped green bell pepper**
- **1 cup sliced celery**
- **12 ounces diced ham**
- **1 teaspoon dried thyme**
- **½ teaspoon rubbed sage**
- **1 bay leaf, crushed**
- **½ teaspoon black pepper**
- **½ teaspoon white pepper**
- **¼ teaspoon cayenne pepper**
- **1 14½ ounce can diced tomatoes, or 2 cups diced fresh tomato**
- **3 tablespoons olive oil**
- **½ cup dry white wine**
- **½ teaspoon salt**

Rinse the beans and place them in a saucepan with the 6 cups of water. Bring the pot to a boil, simmer for about 10 minutes, cover and let the beans soak while you are preparing the other ingredients.

Place the chopped onion, bell pepper, celery, diced ham, thyme, sage, bay leaf, the three peppers, diced tomato and olive oil in the slow cooker. Add the soaked beans and cook on high for 5 hours or low for 9–10 hours. Remove 3 cups of the soup from the crock to a blender and puree. Return it to the crock along with the white wine and salt. Adjust the seasoning and cook for an additional 30 minutes (high) or 1 hour (low).

Joe supports the family businesses.

Chef's Notes: *For another day of the week, try this same recipe with Great Northern White Beans.*

WINE SUGGESTION: White—a Viognier or a Gewurztraminer. Red—a Pinot Noir or a medium bodied Zinfandel.

Mock Turtle Soup

SERVES 8

"IS IT AN EARTHQUAKE, OR SIMPLY A SHOCK? Is it the real Turtle Soup, or merely the mock?" Joe's cousin, Melvin Poché loves that song. Melvin never married, and lives in a fabulous condo in the lower French Quarter. His roommate, Butch, make the most divine soups, and this one is to die for.

½ cup butter
½ cup flour
2 cups chopped onion
1 cup chopped bell pepper
1 cup chopped celery
1 tablespoon minced garlic
½ teaspoon rosemary
½ teaspoon basil
½ teaspoon thyme
¼ teaspoon cayenne pepper
1 teaspoon black pepper
2 teaspoons salt
¼ teaspoon ground allspice
¼ teaspoon ground cloves
¼ teaspoon ground nutmeg
1 teaspoon grated lemon zest
3 bay leaves, crushed
3 cups beef stock (page 120) or broth
2—2½ pounds chuck roast
2 14½ ounce cans petit diced tomatoes
1 tablespoon Worcestershire sauce
1 tablespoon lemon juice
½ cup dry sherry
2 hard boiled eggs, chopped

Melt the butter in a large, heavy-bottomed pot. Whisk in the flour and cook, stirring frequently, to make a dark brown roux. As soon as the roux is ready, add the chopped onion, bell pepper, and celery and cook, stirring occasionally for 5 minutes. Stir in the next 12 ingredients and cook 1 minute. Add the beef stock and stir until evenly blended in. Pour or ladle the mixture into the slow cooker and add the chuck roast, tomatoes, and Worcestershire sauce. Cover and cook on high for 5–6 hours or low for 10–12 hours.

Remove the chuck roast and dice into about ½ inch cubes. Return it to the crock along with the lemon juice and sherry. Adjust the seasoning and cook

for an additional ½ hour. Serve in large bowls, garnished with chopped hard-boiled eggs, and more sherry if desired.

WINE SUGGESTION: A full-bodied white Burgundy, a California Zinfandel or an Australian Shiraz.

Louisiana State Senate Bean Soup

SERVES 8

DURING HIS HIGH SCHOOL CIVICS CLASS TRIP to our nation's capital, Joe's most memorable impressions of Washington revolved around food—and in particular the famous bean soup served every day at the U. S. Senate Restaurant. He savored its flavor and history, but thought he could cook up a tastier version. A decade later, while serving in the Louisiana legislature, Joe introduced a bill declaring his improved bean soup the "Official Soup of the Louisiana State Senate."

Well, the senators from north Louisiana thought it was too spicy, and those from Cajun country deemed it too "Creole," even though Joe used tasso in the recipe in an attempt to form a Creole-Cajun bloc. Unfortunately, the bill died in committee, but lucky for us, his recipe lives on!

- **1 lb dried navy beans**
- **8 cups water**
- **½ lb tasso**
- **3 bay leaves**
- **4 tablespoons butter**
- **2 cups finely chopped onion**
- **1 tablespoon minced garlic**
- **½ teaspoon white pepper**
- **¼ teaspoon cayenne pepper**
- **1 teaspoon salt (or to taste)**
- **1 tablespoon white wine vinegar**

Combine the beans and the 8 cups of water in a large saucepan and bring it to a boil. Let it simmer, uncovered, for 10 minutes, then remove the pot from the heat. Cover the pot and let the beans soak for 1 hour while preparing the other ingredients.

Place the soaked beans and water in the crock along with the tasso and bay leaves. Cook on low for 6–7 hours. Remove the bay leaves and discard. Remove the tasso, cool and chop into an approximately ¼-inch dice. Remove ¼ cup of the beans and mash them into a smooth paste, return to the crock and stir well.

The toque of the town.

Melt the butter in a large skillet. Add the chopped onions and sauté over a medium-high heat, stirring frequently, for 10 minutes until soft and lightly browned. Add the garlic, white pepper, cayenne pepper and salt. Cook one minute more. Add this to the crock along with the chopped tasso, and vinegar. Stir to mix and continue cooking on low for an additional hour.

Chef's Notes: *If you have a hard time finding tasso, just use ½ lb smoked ham instead, and add a little more cayenne pepper.*

WINE SUGGESTION: None. Louisiana State Senators do not drink while they are in session.

1
2
Slow Joe.
SLOW.
YUM
3

Entrées

NOTHING ROUNDS OUT A GOOD MEAL like an entrée. People in Spain or California may enjoy a meal of appetizer sized dishes, which can be quite delicious, but down here people tend to like at least one course to be large. The entrées in this chapter also reflect the multitude of ethnic influences on the New Orleans menu.

Cajun Jambalaya with Sausage and Pork

SERVES 8

"JAMBALAYA, CRAWFISH PIE, FILÉ GUMBO"—Joe's Cajun friend Boudreaux used to sing that song endlessly every time he got drunk. It drove Joe crazy, so he challenged Boudreaux to a jambalaya cook off. If Joe won, Boudreaux would never again sing the tormenting tune in Joe's presence. If Boudreaux triumphed, he would continue his drunken concerts, and Joe would agree to sing harmony, plus let Boudreaux throw in an old Cajun joke between verses—and Joe would have to laugh, like some silly sidekick. Elders of the local Jambalaya Festival would judge the event.

The stakes were high but Joe had confidence, plus he "knew something" about one of the judge's sons. Needless to say, Joe won and Boudreaux piped down. Here's the winning recipe, adapted for the slow cooker.

2 tablespoons butter or bacon drippings
1 lb lean pork, cubed
2 cups chopped onion
1 cup chopped bell pepper
4 cloves garlic, minced
1 teaspoon salt
1 teaspoon cayenne pepper
½ teaspoon black pepper
3½ cups beef stock (page 120) or broth
2 bay leaves, crushed
1 lb smoked sausage, sliced
1 lb smoked ham, cubed
2 cups converted long grain rice

Heat the butter or bacon drippings in a skillet set over a high heat and brown the cubed pork. Transfer the pork to the slow cooker, leaving any drippings in the skillet. Add the chopped onion and bell pepper to the skillet and cook over high heat, stirring often, for about 10 minutes or until onions have browned. Add the garlic, salt, cayenne pepper, and black pepper, stir and cook for 1 minute. Remove the pan from the heat and add the beef broth or stock, stirring to deglaze the pan. Transfer the contents of the pan to the slow cooker along with the bay leaves, sausage, and ham. Cook on

high for 2½–3 hours or low for 5–6 hours. If cooking on low, switch to high, stir in the converted rice, cover and cook for one hour until rice is tender and all liquid is absorbed.

Chef's Notes: *This is a Cajun style jambalaya, popular in southwest Louisiana and brown in color. A Creole or New Orleans style jambalaya would generally contain tomatoes and include shrimp and/or chicken.*

WINE SUGGESTION: A California chardonnay would work with this, or if you're in the mood for red, try a French Côtes du Rhône or an Australian Shiraz.

Boudreaux walked into a bar with a priest, a rabbi, an Irishman, and a duck. The bartender said, "What is this, a joke?"

Creole Jambalaya with Chicken, Sausage, and Shrimp

SERVES 8

- **2 tablespoons butter**
- **2 cups chopped onion**
- **1 cup chopped celery**
- **1 cup chopped bell pepper**
- **3 cloves garlic, minced**
- **1 teaspoon salt**
- **1½ teaspoon cayenne pepper**
- **½ teaspoon black pepper**
- **½ teaspoon white pepper**
- **1 teaspoon thyme**
- **3 bay leaves, crushed**
- **1½ cups seafood stock (page 122) or chicken stock (page 119) or broth**
- **2 14 ounce cans diced tomatoes**
- **1 lb boneless, skinless chicken thighs, cut into bite sized pieces**
- **1 lb smoked sausage, sliced**
- **2 cups converted long grain rice**
- **¼ cup chopped parsley**
- **1 lb peeled medium-size shrimp**

Heat the butter in a skillet set over a high heat and sauté the chopped onion, celery and bell pepper, stirring often, for about 5 minutes or until onions are translucent. Add the garlic, salt, black pepper, white pepper, cayenne pepper, and bay leaves, stir and cook for 1 minute. Remove the pan from the heat and add the stock or broth, stirring to deglaze the pan. Transfer the contents of the pan to the slow cooker along with the diced tomatoes, chicken, and sausage. Cook on high for 2½–3 hours or low for 5–6 hours. If cooking on low, switch to high, stir in the converted rice, parsley, and shrimp, cover and cook for one hour until rice is tender and all liquid is absorbed.

Chef's Notes: *If you are using frozen shrimp, be sure to let them thoroughly thaw before adding to the crock.*

WINE SUGGESTION: A Sauvignon Blanc, Sancerre, white Bordeaux, or Gewurztraminer. If you must have red, try a Beaujolais, a Chianti, or a light bodied Pinot Noir.

Shrimp Creole

5–6 SERVINGS

TO DEVELOP THE TRUE NEW ORLEANS FLAVOR of this delicious traditional dish, the tomatoes and onions have to really cook down and caramelize a bit. Joe likes to use a large 6 quart cooker, even though the recipe yields only 5 or 6 servings. Cooking a small volume of food in a large cooker puts a greater percentage of the food in direct contact with the heated surface of the crock, resulting in the browning that creates such great depth of flavor.

½ cup butter
⅓ cup flour
1½ cup chopped onion
¾ cup chopped celery
¾ cup chopped bell pepper
½ teaspoon black pepper
½ teaspoon white pepper
¼ teaspoon cayenne pepper
2 bay leaves
½ teaspoon thyme
½ teaspoon basil
1 teaspoon salt
1 cup tomato sauce
2 cups diced tomatoes (or 1—14½ oz can)
2 pounds raw peeled shrimp, medium size
¼ cup chopped parsley

Melt the butter in a heavy bottomed pan over a medium high heat. Add the flour and cook, stirring often, until you have a medium brown roux. Add the onion, celery and bell pepper and cook, stirring occasionally, for 6–8 minutes. Add the black pepper, white pepper, cayenne pepper, bay leaves, thyme, basil, salt, and the tomato sauce. Stir to mix and cook for one minute. Place the contents of the pan in the crock along with the diced tomatoes, stir and cook on low for 4 hours.

Remove the lid and stir well. Some of the sauce will probably be stuck to the sides of the crock and look almost as if it were burned. This is good—it's the caramelization process mentioned above. Just scrape all the stuck stuff from the sides of the crock and stir it into the sauce. Add the shrimp and parsley and continue cooking on low for 1 hour, stirring once during the cooking if possible.

Serve over steamed rice.

Chef's Notes: *Cooked properly, as described above, this is an awesome dish. Unfortunately, there are many second-rate recipes for Shrimp Creole floating around. Don't be fooled! Also, make sure you use good quality shrimp. Frozen is okay, as long as they are wild caught Gulf of Mexico shrimp purchased from a reputable dealer.*

WINE SUGGESTION: A Sancerre from France or a California Sauvignon Blanc.

A big Mardi Gras fan since the flambeau-lit, glass-beaded parades of childhood, Joe always wondered how kids in other parts of the country made it through February. He also spent time in the school library researching other culture's carnivals, including those of Rio de Janeiro, Trinidad, Big Mamou, and Mobile. Classmate and fellow library rat Angela Gagliano used to tell Joe wildly fabricated tales of the famous carnival in Venice. Intrigued, early one Mardi Gras morning Joe set off for that tiny fishing village near the mouth of the river, only to suffer stinging humiliation at his geographical gullibility. He did, however, score a fine pair of white shrimp boots, and managed to return to New Orleans in time to watch Comus meet Rex on television.

Smothered Okra with Shrimp

SERVES 5–6

THIS DISH IS A REGULAR with the Simmer household. Sometimes referred to as "dry gumbo," it's quite tasty and a fairly common New Orleans home cooked meal.

- **1/4 cup olive oil**
- **3 cups chopped onion**
- **1/2 cup chopped celery**
- **3/4 teaspoon salt**
- **1 teaspoon black pepper**
- **1/2 teaspoon white pepper**
- **1/4 teaspoon cayenne pepper**
- **1/2 teaspoon dried thyme**
- **1 teaspoon flour**
- **1 tablespoon minced garlic**
- **1 bay leaf, crushed**
- **1 14 1/2 ounce can diced tomatoes**
- **1/2 cup dry white wine**
- **2 lbs sliced okra, fresh or frozen**
- **1 lb peeled, deveined shrimp, about 50–60 count**

Heat the olive oil in a large skillet set over a high heat. Add the chopped onion and celery and sauté, stirring often for about 10 minutes, or until the onions have browned. Combine the salt, three peppers, thyme and flour. Sprinkle the mixture onto the browned onions, add the garlic and the bay leaf, stir and cook for 1 minute. Stir in the diced tomatoes and white wine and remove the pan form the heat.

Place the sliced okra in the slow cooker. Pour the contents of the skillet over the okra, stir to mix, cover and cook on low for 2–2 1/2 hours, until okra is tender but still holds it shape. Stir in the peeled shrimp and continue cooking on low for 1 additional hour.

Serve over steamed rice.

Chef's Notes: *This dish can also be prepared with sliced smoked sausage or cubed, cooked boneless chicken instead of, or in addition to the shrimp.*

WINE SUGGESTION: Anything from France's Loire Valley or a crisp California Sauvignon Blanc.

Crawfish Etouffée

SERVES 6

JOE'S CAJUN COUSIN ON HIS MOTHER'S SIDE, Jenearl Simeneaux, is named after her mother, Joe's aunt Jennie, and her father, Uncle Earl. They lived on a houseboat on Bayou Lafourche, near Raceland, where Joe spent many a summer weekend during his youth. Jenearl was a strange girl—not wrapped too tight—and she fancied Joe. She would spend all day peeling a trap full of fresh crawfish, and then smother them down in onions and peppers just to watch Joe smile and lick his lips with that first bite. The whole thing kind of freaked him out, but he humored her just long enough to get the recipe.

- **½ cup plus 1 tablespoon butter, separated**
- **½ cup flour**
- **4 cups chopped onion**
- **1 cup chopped bell pepper**
- **1 cup chopped celery**
- **1 tablespoon minced garlic**
- **1 teaspoon black pepper**
- **1 teaspoon white pepper**
- **¼ teaspoon cayenne pepper**
- **1 teaspoon salt**
- **3 teaspoons paprika**
- **1 cup chicken stock**
- **2 pounds peeled crawfish tails**
- **½ cup green onion**
- **¼ cup chopped parsley**
- **1 tablespoon fresh lemon juice**

In a heavy bottomed pot or large saucepan, melt ½ cup of butter, whisk in the flour and cook over a medium high heat, stirring almost constantly with the wire whisk and make a medium brown roux. Add the onion,bell pepper, celery, and garlic. Stir to mix and remove the pan from the heat. Stir in the black, white and cayenne peppers, salt, paprika and chicken stock. Transfer everything to the slow cooker and cook on low for 3 hours.

Stir the sauce well. Don't worry if some of the sauce is browned and stuck to the sides of the crock. This process develops great flavor—just scrape off any stuck particles and mix them into the sauce. Add the peeled crawfish tails, green onion, parsley, lemon juice, and the remaining 1 tablespoon of butter. Stir to mix and cook on low for 1 hour.

Serve over steamed rice.

Chef's Notes: *For best results, use fresh, un-rinsed Louisiana crawfish tails. Frozen is okay, as long as they have been frozen only 3 months or less.*

WINE SUGGESTION: Try a crisp white Bordeaux, a flinty Sauvignon Blanc, or perhaps a dry Alsatian Riesling.

Some like it hot. Joe likes it slow.

Chicken Sauce Piquante

SERVES 6–8

- **3 lbs boneless, skinless chicken thighs**
- **1 teaspoon salt**
- **½ teaspoon black pepper**
- **½ teaspoon white pepper**
- **¼ teaspoon cayenne pepper**
- **⅓ cup olive oil**
- **¼ cup flour**
- **2 cups chopped onion**
- **1 cup chopped green bell pepper**
- **1 cup chopped celery**
- **1 tablespoon minced garlic**
- **1 fresh jalapeño pepper, minced**
- **1 cup canned crushed tomato**
- **1 14½ ounce can diced tomatoes**
- **¼ teaspoon Tabasco sauce**

Cut the chicken into strips, approximately 1-inch by 2-inches. Combine the salt and three peppers and season the chicken strips. Set aside.

In a large, heavy bottomed saucepan, heat the olive oil over a high heat. Whisk in the flour and cook, stirring constantly, to make a light-to-medium brown roux—about the color of peanut butter or a little lighter. Immediately add the chopped onion, bell pepper, and celery, reduce the heat to medium-high and cook for 5 minutes, stirring often. Stir in the minced garlic and jalapeño and cook 1 minute.

Transfer the mixture to the slow cooker and add the crushed tomato, diced tomatoes, Tabasco sauce, and the seasoned chicken. Stir to mix, cover, and cook on high for 3½ hours or low for 7 hours.

Serve over steamed rice.

Chef's Notes: *For the bold, this dish can also be prepared with alligator, which tastes like chicken. Use the white tail meat.*

WINE SUGGESTION: A light red or a hearty white.

Chicken Fricassée

SERVES 6–8

THE TERM "FRICASSÉE" comes from the French word "fricassée" which is translated as "fricassée", and is the feminine noun derived from the transitive verb "fricasser" meaning "to cook chopped food in its own juice". Man, that Joe he knows some stuff!

- **2½ lbs boneless, skinless chicken thighs**
- **Salt and pepper to taste**
- **Flour for dredging**
- **4 tablespoons butter**
- **1 cup finely chopped onion**
- **1 cup sliced green onion**
- **1 bay leaf, crushed**
- **1 tablespoon minced fresh parsley**
- **½ teaspoon thyme**
- **¼ teaspoon allspice**
- **¼ teaspoon mace**
- **1 tablespoon Worcestershire sauce**
- **2 cups chicken broth or stock**

Season the chicken thighs with salt and pepper and dredge in the flour, shaking off any excess. Melt the butter in a larger skillet set over a medium-high heat. Quickly sauté the chicken until medium brown on both sides, and transfer the thighs in the crock. Add the chopped onion to the pan, cook 1 minute and scrape them into the crock along with any browned bits stuck to the bottom of the pan. Add all remaining ingredients and cook on high for 3½ hours or low for 6–7 hours.

Serve over steamed rice.

WINE SUGGESTION: A red Burgundy or Côtes du Rhône, or a California Pinot Noir or Syrah.

Chicken Etouffée

SERVES 8

THIS DISH STANDS ON ITS OWN AS DELICIOUS—not some lame, second-rate rendition of Crawfish Etouffée. Try it!

- **½ cup butter**
- **½ cup flour**
- **5 cups chopped onion**
- **1 cup chopped green bell pepper**
- **1 cup chopped celery**
- **1 tablespoon minced garlic**
- **1 teaspoon black pepper**
- **1 teaspoon white pepper**
- **½ teaspoon cayenne pepper**
- **1 teaspoon salt**
- **1 tablespoon paprika**
- **1½ cups chicken stock (page 119) or broth**
- **3 lbs boneless, skinless chicken thighs, cut into 1-inch cubes**
- **1 cup sliced green onions**
- **¼ cup chopped parsley**

Melt the butter in a large, heavy bottomed pot set over a medium-high heat. Whisk in the flour and cook, stirring constantly to make a light-to-medium brown roux—about the color of peanut butter or a little lighter. Immediately add the chopped onion, bell pepper and celery. Reduce the heat to medium, and cook, stirring often, for 10 minutes. Stir in the garlic, the three peppers, salt and paprika, and cook 1 minute. Add the chicken stock and stir to mix. Bring the mixture to a boil, stirring often.

Transfer the contents of the pot to the slow cooker and add the cubed chicken. Stir to mix, cover and cook on high for 3 hours or low for 6 hours. Stir in the sliced green onion and chopped parsley, adjust the seasoning and cook, covered for an additional 5–10 minutes.

Serve over steamed rice.

This slow food sure beats fast food.

Chef's Notes: *The sauce will appear quite thick when first transferred to the crock. As it cooks a lot of moisture will come out of the large quantity of chopped onion, resulting in a sauce or proper consistency.*

WINE SUGGESTION: A big California Chardonnay without too much oak, or a delicious white Burgundy.

Chicken Bonne Femme

SERVES 6

- **3 lbs chicken thighs and legs, skinned**
- **½ teaspoon black pepper**
- **½ teaspoon white pepper**
- **¼ teaspoon cayenne pepper**
- **1 teaspoon salt**
- **Flour for dredging**
- **2 tablespoons butter**
- **2 cups chopped onion**
- **½ cup chopped garlic**
- **¾ cup white wine**
- **1 teaspoon dried thyme**
- **1 teaspoon dried basil**
- **1 lb white mushrooms, wiped clean and cut into quarters**
- **1 14 ounce can quartered artichoke hearts, drained and rinsed**
- **½ cup chopped fresh parsley**

Combine the salt and peppers and season the skinless chicken parts. Dredge the chicken in the flour, shaking off any excess. Melt the butter in a large skillet set over a medium-high heat and brown the chicken. Set aside.

In the same skillet, sauté the chopped onion, stirring often, for about 5 minutes. Add the garlic and cook for 1 minute. Stir in the wine, thyme and basil and remove the pan from the heat.

Place the quartered mushrooms and artichoke hearts in the crock. Arrange the browned chicken pieces on top, then pour the contents of the skillet over all. Cover and cook or low for 6–7 hours or high for 3–3½ hours. Add the chopped parsley, stir gently and cook, covered, for an additional 5 minutes.

WINE SUGGESTION: Matching wine with a dish containing artichokes is always a challenge, due to the vegetable's inherent tannins. Try a Sancerre or a Pouilly-Fumé, or perhaps a crisp, acidic Italian white.

JOE'S CHICK

Stewed Hen

SERVES 6–8

JOE RECENTLY ENJOYED a stewed hen at the queen's supper when his cousin (on his mother's side) Martine "Miffy" Simone Villere Latour Claiborne made her debut this past carnival season. Joe observed that the current year's crop of debs seemed bred with the ability to consume huge quantities of inexpensive liquor, and, mystically, still behave "like ladies"—at least in the eyes of the like-minded gentlemen to whom they were presented.

1 roasting hen, about 6 lbs
4 strips thick sliced bacon
3 medium onions, cut in half and sliced
4 clove garlic, thinly sliced
1 teaspoon salt
1 teaspoon black pepper
1 large lemon, sliced
1 teaspoon poultry seasoning
3 bay leaves, crushed
1 cup chicken broth or stock

Set a skillet over a medium-high heat and fry the bacon until most of the fat is rendered out, but it's not too crisp. Chop into 1-inch pieces and set aside. Skin the chicken and cut it into pieces, cutting each breast into 3 pieces and each thigh into 2 pieces. Save the wings and back for stock.

Place the chicken in the crock and surround it with the bacon, onions and garlic. Distribute the seasonings and lemon slices over the chicken. Gently pour in the broth or stock. Cook for 4 hours on high or 7–8 hours on low.

Serve with steamed rice.

• •

WINE SUGGESTION: Chicken is easy–Chardonnay, Merlot or Pinot Noir.

***A** recent study revealed that if the interbreeding of the New Orleans social elite was to continue, in another generation or so there would be no need for Rex's Mardi Gras night procession to the adjoining ballroom to meet Comus, as they would already be joined at the hip.*

Macque Choux Chicken

SERVES 6–8

- **1 cup unbleached flour**
- **1½ teaspoons salt**
- **1 teaspoon black pepper**
- **3 lbs boneless, skinless chicken thighs**
- **4 tablespoons olive oil**
- **2 cups coarsely chopped onion**
- **½ cup chopped bell pepper**
- **4 cloves minced garlic**
- **1 14½ ounce can chopped tomatoes**
- **1½ cups chicken broth**
- **1 pound frozen whole kernel corn**
- **1 14½ ounce can creamed corn**
- **½ cup sliced green onion tops**

Combine the flour, salt and pepper in a large bowl and mix well. Dredge the chicken thighs in the flour mixture so they are evenly coated, shaking off any excess.

In a large skillet, heat the olive oil over a medium-high heat and quickly brown the chicken on both sides, setting the thighs in the slow cooker as they are browned. Add the onions and bell peppers to the skillet and sauté for about 3 minutes.

Scrape the sautéed onions and peppers into the slow cooker. Add all remaining ingredients except the sliced green onion tops. Cook on high for 3½ hours or low for 7 hours, stirring once during the cooking if possible.

Serve in large bowls and garnish with sliced green onion tops.

Chef's Notes: *Be sure to scrape up all the flavorful caramelized bits stuck to the bottom of the skillet. Try deglazing the pan with the chicken broth to get the most out of it.*

WINE SUGGESTION: Beer.

Creole Coq Au Vin

SERVES 6

A FAVORITE FROM THE MOTHER COUNTRY, just a bit more garlic and spice.

- **4 strips thick cut bacon, cross cut into ¼-inch pieces**
- **4 lbs chicken thighs and legs, skinned**
- **½ teaspoon salt**
- **½ teaspoon black pepper**
- **½ teaspoon white pepper**
- **¼ teaspoon cayenne pepper**
- **1 cup chopped onion**
- **½ cup chopped carrots**
- **3 tablespoons flour**
- **2 cups red wine**
- **2 tablespoons tomato paste**
- **1 teaspoon thyme**
- **3 bay leaves, crushed**
- **½ lb sliced mushrooms**
- **½ cup peeled garlic cloves, about 25**
- **½ cup red wine**
- **¼ cup chopped parsley**

In a large skillet set over a medium heat, cook the bacon until browned but not too crisp. Set aside. Meanwhile, combine the salt and three peppers and season the chicken. Brown the seasoned chicken in the bacon drippings and set aside.

Sauté the onion and carrots in the bacon drippings for 5–7 minutes, or until onions are tender. Stir in the flour and cook for 5 minutes, stirring often. Add the wine, tomato paste, thyme and bay leaves and bring to a boil, stirring constantly. Remove the pan from the heat.

Place the mushrooms and garlic in the crock. Sprinkle in the bacon pieces. Arrange the browned chicken on top and pour the contents of the skillet over all. Cook on high for 3 hours or low for 6 hours. Adjust the seasoning, add the chopped parsley and ½ cup of red wine and cook on high for an additional 10 minutes.

WINE SUGGESTION: Something French would be appropriate, like a Puligny-Montrachet or Meursault (white) or a medium bodied Burgundy or "Crus Bourgeois" Bordeaux (red).

New Orleans Creole Italian Red Gravy

MAKES ABOUT $3\frac{1}{2}$ QUARTS

JOE LOVED THE MULTI-ETHNIC NEIGHBORHOOD of his childhood—a "cultural crock pot" you may dare say. Best friend Manny Mancuso's mama used to make the best red gravy and spaghetti with Italian sausage. During one Saturday afternoon sausage eating contest, Manny, who was skinny, downed 17 links in 49 seconds, earning his life-long nickname "Lil' Sausage."

This sauce freezes well, and can be used for meat balls, meatloaf, pot roast, just by itself over spaghetti, or of course with Italian sausage.

½ cup olive oil
6 cups finely chopped onion
2 tablespooons minced garlic
1 teaspoon dried basil
½ teaspooon black pepper
¼ teaspoon white pepper
⅛ teaspoon cayenne pepper
3 29 ounce cans tomato puree
3 cups water
1 teaspoon salt
½ cup chopped fresh basil

Heat the olive oil in a large skillet over a medium heat. Add the onions and sauté, stirring occasionally for about 20 minutes, or until the onion are translucent but not browned. Add the garlic, dried basil, and the three peppers and cook for 5 more minutes.

Transfer the contents of the pan to the slow cooker and add the tomato puree, water, and salt. Stir until evenly mixed and set the cooker on high for 10 hours. If possible, stir once or twice during the cooking process.

After 10 hours, add the fresh basil, adjust the seasoning, and if it is too thick add a little water. Stir to mix and cook an additional 15 minutes.

Chef's Notes: *Use the best quality tomato puree you can get your hands on. Italian markets usually carry imported brands available in flexible cartons*

Joe's friend eats a sausage po-boy overflowing with Red Gravy.

that are good. Several domestic brands are packed in cans with enamel linings, which eliminates the metallic taste sometimes found in lesser brands.

• •

VARIATIONS: Manny's mama's sister-in-law Ronnie Ragosa makes her red gravy with wine instead of water. Both women will politely eat each other's sauce, then after a few glasses of wine, comment that it is "good" but not the "real" red gravy. After a few more Chiantis, it gets nasty. Like the time Mr. Ragosa had to bring his wife home after her crude comment pondering the "real" reason for Manny's moniker "Lil' Sausage."

Joe likes both versions. Just substitute 1½–2 cups of dry red wine for an equal amount of water.

Meatballs and Spaghetti

SERVES 6

MEATBALLS AND SPAGHETTI—what can Joe say?

- **1½ lbs lean ground beef**
- **½–¾ cups fine dry bread crumbs**
- **½ cup finely chopped onion**
- **½ cup finely chopped celery**
- **1 tablespoon minced garlic**
- **2 tablespoons chopped parsley**
- **2 eggs, beaten**
- **1 teaspoon black pepper**
- **¼ teaspoon cayenne pepper**
- **1 teaspoon salt**
- **2 teaspoons dried basil**
- **½ teaspoon dreid oregano**
- **½ cup grated Parmesan cheese**
- **1 tablespoon olive oil**
- **3 cups Creole Italian Red Gravy (page 60)**
- **1 lb good quality dried spaghetti**

Pre-heat the oven to 400º. While the oven is heating, combine the first 13 ingredients (everything except the olive oil, red gravy, and spaghetti) in a large bowl and mix well. Shape the mixture into twelve 2-inch meatballs. Lightly oil a cookie sheet or flat baking pan with some of the olive oil. Using your hands, coat each ball with a bit of the oil and place them on the pan, being careful not to let them touch each other. Bake for 10 minutes.

Pour 1 cup of the Creole Italian Red Gravy into slow cooker. Gently position all the balls in the crock. Top with the remaining 2 cups of red gravy. Cover and cook on low for 6 hours or high for 3 hours.

Prepare the spaghetti according to package directions. Serve as you would serve meatballs and spaghetti.

Chef's Notes: *If available, a nice finishing touch is about ½ cup of chopped fresh basil stirred into the sauce a few minutes before serving, and additional chopped basil to sprinkle on top of each serving at the table.*

WINE SUGGESTION: The usual Italian suspects (see Creole Daube and Spaghetti, page 64), or a California Sangiovese or Pinot Noir.

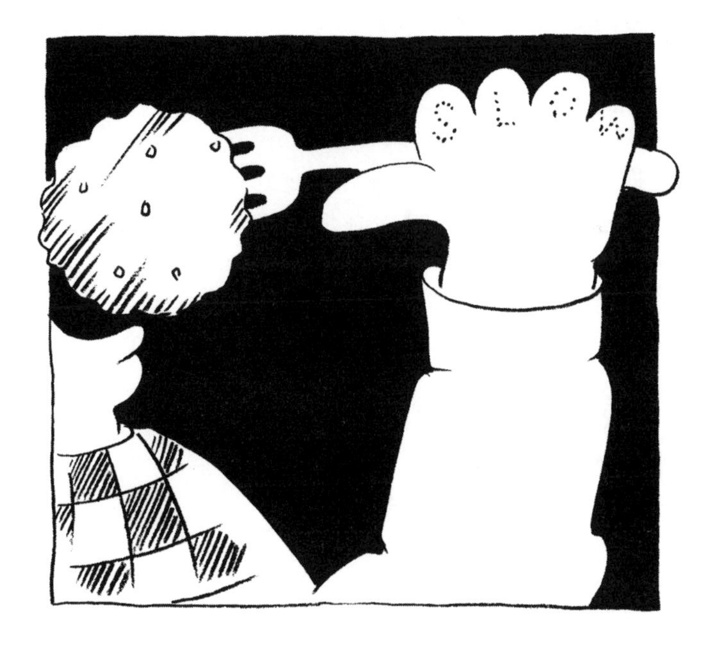

Creole Spaghetti and Daube

SERVES 6–8

THE WORD "*DAUBE*" COME FROM THE FRENCH WORD "DAUBIÈRE," translated as a covered casserole or stew, and popular in the Provence region of France. How this ends up as an old New Orleans Creole Italian favorite is just one of those strange "cultural crock pot" things.

2½–3 lb rump roast
½ teaspoon salt
½ teaspoon black pepper
½ teaspoon white pepper
½ teaspoon cayenne pepper
1 tablespooon olive oil
½ cup red wine
2 cups Creole Italian Red Gravy (page 60)
1 lb good quality dried spaghetti

Combine the salt and peppers and rub the mixture into the roast. Heat the olive oil in a large skillet set over a high heat and quickly brown the meat on all sides. Place the roast in the slow cooker.

Pour the red wine into skillet and bring it to a boil while scraping up any bits and particles stuck to the bottom of the pan. Add the red gravy and stir until evenly mixed, then pour it over the roast in the crock. Lift up the roast to allow some of the gravy to get under it, then cover and cook on high for 5–6 hours. If possible, baste once or twice during the cooking.

Prepare the spaghetti according to package directions. Remove the roast from the crock and let it cool a bit while the spaghetti is cooking. Transfer the sauce to a skillet set over a high heat, and boil, stirring often, to reduce the gravy to desired thickness.

Slice the roast and serve it on plates next to the spaghetti, topping both with a little gravy.

WINE SUGGESTION: Barbaresco, Barolo, Barbera, or Chianti Classico Riserva.

Pot Roast Courtbouillon

SERVES 6

INTERESTINGLY, THIS CLASSIC REDFISH PREPARATION works quite well with beef—possibly even better, as the beef is not overwhelmed by the bold flavors of the sauce.

- **1 chuck roast, about 3 lbs**
- **1 teaspoon salt**
- **½ teaspoon black pepper**
- **½ teaspoon white pepper**
- **¼ teaspoon cayenne pepper**
- **¼ teaspoon ground allspice**
- **¼ teaspoon nutmeg**
- **2 tablespoons olive oil**
- **2 cups chopped onion**
- **1 cup chopped green bell pepper**
- **1 cup chopped celery**
- **3 bay leaves, crushed**
- **1 tablespoon minced garlic**
- **1 14½ ounce can diced tomatoes**
- **½ cup red wine**
- **¾ cup beef stock (page 120) or broth**

Trim any excess fat from the roast and discard it. Combine the salt, peppers, allspice, and nutmeg and rub the mixture into the meat. Heat the olive oil in a skillet over a high heat and quickly brown the roast on all sides. Position the meat in the center of the crock.

Lower the heat under the skillet to medium-high and add the chopped onion, bell pepper, and celery. Sauté, stirring frequently, for about 10 minutes. Stir in the bay leaves and garlic and cook 1 minute. Add the tomatoes, wine, and beef stock and stir to mix. Pour the contents of the skillet over the roast, then lift the roast enough to let some of the liquid under it, then set it back in place. Cover and cook on high for 4–5 hours or low for 8–10 hours, or until meat is tender.

WINE SUGGESTION: A full bodied California Syrah or Zinfandel or an Australian Syrah/Cabernet blend.

Grillades and Grits

SERVES 6

THE FRENCH WORD *"GRILLADE"* translates as "grilled meat," but this favorite New Orleans brunch dish is prepared by braising veal or beef round, or by Joe's hand, quickly browning and slow cooking. While Joe loves Grillades and Grits, he never was a big brunch fan. Thinking it too much food and drink for so early in the day, he much prefers what he terms "dunch"—a mid to late afternoon repast enjoyed between the traditional times for lunch and dinner.

2 lbs beef top round, sliced ½-inch thick
Salt
Black pepper
Flour for dredging
¼ cup butter
1½ cups chopped onion
1½ cups chopped green bell pepper
½ cup chopped celery
1 14½ ounce can petite diced tomato
1 cup beef stock or broth
½ cup red wine
½ teaspoon dried thyme
¼ teaspoon salt
⅛ teaspoon cayenne pepper
1 bay leaf, crushed
2 tablespoons chopped parsley

Cut the meat into strips approximately 1½ inches by 4 inches. Season the strips with salt and black pepper and coat with flour. Melt the butter in a large skillet and quickly brown the meat on both sides. Set aside.

Add the chopped onion, bell pepper, and celery to the drippings remaining in the skillet and cook for about three minutes, stirring frequently. Turn off the heat and stir in the diced tomatoes. Transfer the contents of the skillet to the slow cooker and add the beef stock, red wine, thyme, bay leaf, cayenne pepper, and salt. Stir to mix, and distribute the browned meat strips on top. Cover and cook on low for 4 hours.

Add the chopped parsley, stir gently and adjust the seasoning. Hold the grillades on the "keep warm" setting while you prepare the grits according to package directions, allowing them to cook a little longer, leaning a bit to the thick side.

Chef's Notes: *If grits are not you cup of tea, this dish does well with rice also.*

WINE SUGGESTION: A classy claret would be lovely, but any big, full bodied Cabernet Sauvignon, Merlot, Malbec, Zinfandel, or Syrah would work.

Dans le monde de la cuisine lente, voila le maître, M. Simmer! Son livre de recettes est vraiment magnifique! Laissez les bon temps roullez a Paris aussi, mes amis!

—JACQUE DE MAUREPAS
Societe de la Cuisine Lente
Paris, France

Osso Boudreaux

SERVES 4

JOE'S CRAZY FRIEND BOUDREAUX used to work out on the oil rigs as a wrench-swinging roustabout, working one week on, two weeks off. Once while doing some day labor on a visiting tanker during an off week, Boudreaux fell asleep on the job (probably drunk) and woke up in the port of Genoa, Italy. While he was wandering around in a daze mumbling Cajun French nonsense, a sympathetic Italian family took pity and took him in for a few days. They brought him to their villa near Milan, explained his whereabouts, and fed him lots of Osso Buco. Boudreaux appreciated their hospitality, and enjoyed the tasty braised veal shanks—though delicious he knew he could "kick it up a notch."

Upon his return to Louisiana, Boudreaux had Joe over for dinner, told tales of his tour of the continent, and prepared, for the very first time in the new world, Osso Boudreaux.

4 veal shanks, cut 1½ inches thick, about 3 lbs
1 teaspoon black pepper
¼ teaspoon cayenne pepper
¼ teaspoon salt
2 tablespoons olive oil
½ cup chopped onion
½ cups diced carrots
½ cup chopped celery
12 whole peeled garlic cloves
3 bay leaves, crushed
½ teaspoon dried thyme
2 tablespoons flour
1 cup chicken stock (page 119) or broth
1 cup dry white wine
3 tablespoons chopped parsley
3 cloves garlic, minced
1 teaspoon grated lemon zest
3 cups cooked yellow grits

Combine the peppers and salt and rub it into the veal shanks. Heat the olive oil in a skillet set over a high heat and quickly brown the shanks on both sides. Transfer the browned shanks to the slow cooker.

Add the onions, carrots and celery to the skillet and cook, stirring often for 5 minutes. Stir in the garlic, bay leaves, thyme and flour and cook for 1 minute. Add the chicken stock and wine and stir to mix. Pour the contents of the skillet over the veal shanks and cook on low for 6 hours or high for 3 hours.

Combine the parsley, garlic and lemon zest. Mix well and set aside. Shortly before the shanks are done, prepare the grits according to package directions, but cooking them a little longer so they are thick—not runny.

Serve the veal shanks and grits on a plate, with some gravy over the grits, and sprinkle the parsley-garlic-lemon zest mixture over all.

WINE SUGGESTION: A Barbera or Chianti Classico would be a good choice of reds, and a dry Alsace Gewurztraminer an interesting white selection.

Corned Beef and Cabbage

SERVES 6

MOST OF THE INGREDIENTS IN THIS RECIPE can be caught from a passing float in the annual Irish Channel Saint Patrick's Day parade.

By the time Joe came of age, New Orleans' Irish Channel existed as a multicultural neighborhood, as the descendents of the original Irish immigrants had mostly moved either "on up" or to the suburbs. But every year in mid-March, the progeny of the old inhabitants would come out of the woodwork, or in from the parish, and, along with any other locals who enjoy getting drunk before noon, spend the day at a block party centered around an old neighborhood bar. Green jello shots, green beer, line-dancing office workers, mutant musicians, and has-been politicians all contribute to the sensory overload. These are not your "lace curtain" Irish.

This hearty, homey, spicy recipe reflects the culture of the revelers, and reportedly mitigates the hangover.

- **3 lbs Corned Beef, preferably the lowered sodium variety**
- **1 medium head green cabbage, cored and cut into 8 wedges**
- **3 medium carrots, scrubbed and cut into 1-inch pieces**
- **1 large onion, coarsely chopped**
- **6 cloves garlic, peeled and cut in half**
- **3 bay leaves, crushed**
- **1 teaspoon dried thyme**
- **½ teaspoon black pepper**
- **1½ cup water**
- **1 teaspoon liquid crab boil**
- **12 ounces beer**

Position the cabbage wedges in the bottom of the slow cooker. Distribute the carrots, onion and garlic on top of the cabbage. Add the bay leaves and sprinkle on the thyme and black pepper. Place the corned beef, fat side up, on top, pushing in down into the vegetables if necessary so that it will not touch the lid when covered. Combine the water and liquid crab boil and pour it over the beef along with the beer. Cover and cook on low for 8–10 hours.

Chef's Notes: *While adding a distinctive New Orleans twist, the liquid crab boil makes this dish pretty spicy. If you are "spicy averse," reduce it by half, or eliminate it.*

WINE SUGGESTION: Wine? No wine. Beer, beer, and more beer.

Deep South Pot Roast

SERVES 8–10

- **1 boneless chuck roast, about 4 lbs**
- **Salt and pepper to taste**
- **2 tablespoons olive oil**
- **1 lb carrots, cut into 1-inch pieces**
- **2 lbs russet potatoes, cut into 2-inch cubes**
- **2 cups sliced red onions**
- **1 teaspoon thyme**
- **½ teaspoon ground cloves**
- **3 bay leaves, crushed**
- **1 tablespooon rosemary, crushed**
- **½ cup dry red wine**
- **1 cup beef broth or stock**

Heat the olive oil in a large heavy skillet over a medium-high heat. Season the roast with salt and pepper and brown well on both sides. Place the carrots on the bottom of the slow cooker and center the roast on top. Arrange the potatoes around the sides of the roast and distribute the onion slices over the top. Sprinkle the herbs and spices over all, and gently pour in the red wine and beef stock. Cook on high for 7½ hours.

• •

WINE SUGGESTION: A nice red Bordeaux or a California Cabernet Sauvignon.

Joe's second cousin, Melvin Simmer, was a real yat. He grew up in the old neighborhood but moved out to St. Bernard parish as a yongster, and after finishing junior high school opened a body and fender shop with his stepfather, Mr. Buddy.

After work, Mel would go drink beer with a gang of rough-and-tumble, salt-of-the-earth grease monkeys. At family gatherings he would rib Joe about his sophisticated style and fancy-pants culinary creations, but was jealous of Joe's "way with the ladies," and actually loved his cooking. This was his favorite dish.

Smothered Pork Chops

SERVES 6–8

"POKE CHOPS, POKE CHOPS. Greasy, Greasy.
We'll beat your team, Easy, Easy."

Joe heard a bunch of girls taunting their rivals with this cheer at a recent high school game. Upset about the bad rap that pork chops often get, he created this simple, non-greasy yet delicious recipe.

- **8 center cut pork chops, about 2½–3 lbs**
- **3 tablespoons olive oil**
- **½ cup flour**
- **1 teaspoon salt**
- **1 teaspoon black pepper**
- **4 medium onions, sliced ¼-inch thick**
- **4 garlic cloves, chopped**
- **2 tablespooons chopped parsley**
- **1½ cups chicken broth or stock**

Combine the flour, salt and pepper and mix well. Dredge the chops in the flour mixture, shaking off any excess.

Heat the olive oil in a large heavy skillet over a medium–high heat. Brown the chops on both sides and set aside. Add the onions and garlic to the pan and cook and stir for 3 mintues. Remove the pan from the heat.

Place a layer of onions and garlic in the crock and sprinkle with some of the chopped parsley. Top with a layer of chops and repeat until all chops, onions, garlic and parsley is used. Gently pour in the broth or stock and cook on high for 4½ hours or *low for 7–8 hours.*

Serve with rice or potatoes.

Chef's Notes: *If you would prefer a little more spice, add a teaspoon of white pepper and ½ teaspoon of cayenne pepper to the flour mixture.*

WINE SUGGESTION: If it's cold outside, a California Zinfandel, for warmer weather, a refreshing Sauvignon Blanc.

Southern Pork Loin

SERVES 6–8

1 pork loin, about 3 lbs, trimmed of excess fat
1 teaspoon salt
1 teaspoon black pepper
¼ teaspoon cayenne pepper
1 teaspoon ground sage
1 teaspoon dried thyme
6 cloves garlic, minced
1 tablespoon flour
2 tablespoons butter, divided
3 meduim onions, sliced
3 celery stalks, sliced diagonally, about 1 cup
1 cup chicken stock (page 119) or broth
½ cup red wine

Combine the salt, black pepper, cayenne pepper, sage, thyme, minced garlic and flour and rub it onto all surfaces of the pork loin. Melt 1 tablespoon of the butter in a large skillet or braising pan set over a high heat and brown the seasoned loin on all sides.

Place the loin in the center of the crock. Melt the remaining tablespoon of butter in the skillet, and add the sliced onions and celery. Cook over high heat, stirring frequently, for about 3 minutes. Pour in the chicken stock and remove the pan from the heat.

Evenly distribute the contents of the pan around the meat. Pour in the wine, cover and cook on low for 6–7 hours or high for 3½ hours. If possible, turn the roast over once during the cooking.

Serve with rice or potatoes.

Chef's Notes: *When it comes to wine—as an ingredient or an accompaniment—pork, like chicken, can go either way. Substitute ½ cup dry white wine for the red in this recipe as a subtle variation.*

WINE SUGGESTION: As an ingredient or an accompaniment—a dry Riesling or a Pinot Noir.

This book will certainly effect a shift in the manner of slow cooking, and quite possibly a shift in the manner in which human beings nourish themselves.

—Fant Gender
Culinary Historian

Young Joe rinsing beans.

Beans, Beans, Beans

SLOW COOKERS DO A GREAT JOB ON BEANS, and beans occupy a chunk of shelf space in the Creole pantry. Joe's main method is efficient and effective. Most large beans with thick skins require soaking, and others don't suffer from it. You can soak over night, but if you do it in the refrigerator, the beans are chilled and take too long to heat up in the slow cooker. (Once Joe soaked some red beans overnight on the counter top during a heat wave and the beans sprouted!)

The quick-soak method works very well. Rinse the beans, cover them with water in a saucepan and bring to a boil. Simmer for 10 minute, turn off the heat, cover the pan and let them soak—about an hour if possible—while you prepare the other ingredients for the dish. This way you have a jump-start on your cooking because the beans are already hot. And use the soaking water—there is no reason to throw it away, and it contains nutrients that have leeched out of the beans.

One more note. It's always better to add salt and acidic ingredients such as vinegar, wine, or lemon juice and the end of the cooking process, as these ingredients can prevent the softening of beans.

JS
CREAMERY

Butter Beans and Andouille

SERVES 6–8

SIMPLE TO PREPARE, satisfying and soothing to the soul, this is Creole comfort food at its finest. Though large, butter beans seldom require soaking—so just throw everything in the crock, wait a few hours, and enjoy.

- **1 lb dried large lima beans (butter beans)**
- **4 cups chicken stock (page 119) or broth**
- **1 cup water**
- **1 cup chopped onion**
- **4 cloves garlic, chopped**
- **1 lb sliced Andouille sausage**
- **½ teaspoon salt**
- **1 teaspoon black pepper**
- **3 bay leaves**
- **1 teaspoon thyme**
- **¼ cup chopped parsley (optional)**

Rinse the beans and place them in the crock with all the other ingredients except the parsley. Cook on high for 3½ hours or low for 7 hours. Stir in the parsley, if desired, and serve over steamed rice.

Chef's Notes: *If the dried beans look old and wrinkly, cover them with the water and stock in a saucepan, bring to a boil, cover, turn off the heat and let them soak while preparing the other ingredients.*

WINE SUGGESTION: An Oregon or California Pinot Noir or a French rosé.

Black Eyed Peas with Pickled Pork

SERVES 6–8

LONG BEFORE JOE EVER ACTED ON STAGE, he was an avid reader of plays, and Tennessee Williams reigned as one of his all time favorite playwrights. Reading a tattered old first edition of *Cat on a Hot Tin Roof*, Joe fell head over heels for Maggie, whose wardrobe, it seemed, contained nothing but slips. He was also intrigued with Big Daddy, and his love of "hot buttered biscuits and Hoppin' John." A torn off corner of the page bearing that passage removed the last two letters of "John," and for years Joe thought that the missing page part bore an "e"—and that the famous black eyed pea dish was known as "Hoppin' Joe." A rude disappointment, but it still tastes good.

- **1 lb dried black eyed peas**
- **6 cups water**
- **2 cups finely chopped onion**
- **1 cup finely chopped celery**
- **1 tablespoon minced garlic**
- **1 teaspoon thyme**
- **¼ teaspoon sage**
- **½ teaspoon black pepper**
- **¼ teaspoon cayenne pepper**
- **1 bay leaf**
- **1 pound pickled pork**
- **1 teaspoon salt**
- **1 tablespoon white vinegar**

Rinse the peas and cover them with the 6 cups of water in a large saucepan. Bring to a boil, reduce the heat, and simmer for 10 minutes. Remove from heat, cover, and let them soak while you prepare the other ingredients.

Place the onions, celery, garlic, thyme, sage, the two peppers, and the bay leaf in the crock. Add the soaked beans and stir. Set the pickled pork on top and cook on low for 6 hours.

Remove ¼ cup of peas from the crock and mash them in a small bowl or cup with the back of a spoon. Return them to the crock and add the salt and vinegar. Stir and cook on low for an additional 30 minutes.

Hoppin' Joe and his mean bean-plantin' machine.

Chef's Notes: *This is great with a side of Collards with Red Bell Peppers (page 95) and freshly baked corn bread—or hot buttered biscuits!*

Red Beans and Rice

SERVES 6–8

THIS DISH IS NEW TO JOE as he had not heard of it or tasted it until last year. Just kidding!

- **1 lb dark red kidney beans**
- **6 cups water**
- **2 cups finely chopped onion**
- **1½ cups finely chopped green bell pepper**
- **1 cup finely chopped celery**
- **1 tablespoon minced garlic**
- **3 bay leaves, crushed**
- **1 teaspoon dried thyme**
- **½ teaspoon black pepper**
- **½ teaspoon white pepper**
- **¼ teaspoon cayenne pepper**
- **1 lb smoked sausage, cut into 8 pieces**
- **1 tablespoon vinegar**
- **1½ teaspoons salt, or to taste**
- **2 tablespoons chopped parsley**

Rinse the beans and place them in a large saucepan. Add the water, bring the pot to a boil, lower the heat, and simmer for 10 minutes. Remove the pan form the heat, cover it, and let the beans soak while preparing the other ingredients.

Place the chopped onion, bell pepper, celery, garlic, bay leaves, thyme, the three peppers, and the smoked sausage in the slow cooker. Add the soaked beans and stir to mix. Cover and cook on low for 7 hours or high for 3½ hours, or until beans are tender.

Remove about ¼ cup of beans from the crock to a small bowl. Mash to a smooth paste with the back of a spoon and stir them back in, along with the vinegar, salt, and parsley. Cook on low for about 30 minutes or high for about 15 minutes.

Serve over steamed rice.

Chef's Notes: *Be sure to use beans labeled "dark red kidney beans", and not simply "red beans." The latter lack the deep, almost smoky flavor essential to this dish, and are softer in texture—more like pinto beans.*

Interestingly, most red kidney beans grown in the U.S. come from either Michigan or Colorado—neither place anywhere near the Crescent City.

WINE SUGGESTION: A California or Oregon Pinot Noir is perfect.

White Beans and Collard Greens

SERVES 6–8

SOUL FOOD SO GOOD you'll want to slap someone!

- **1 lb navy beans**
- **4 cups chicken stock (page 119) or broth**
- **1 cup water**
- **1 cup chopped onion**
- **4 cloves garlic, minced**
- **1 lb pickled pork**
- **½ teaspoon salt**
- **1 teaspoon black pepper**
- **3 bay leaves**
- **2 tablespoons olive oil**
- **1 teaspoon thyme**
- **½ lb cleaned, chopped collard greens**

Rinse the beans and place them in a large saucepan along with the broth or stock and the water. Bring the pot to a boil, let it simmer for about 10 minutes, then cover and let soak while preparing the other ingredients.

Cut the pickled pork into 1-inch cubes. Place the pork and all other ingredients, except the collards, into the slow cooker. Add the soaked beans and cook on low for 6 hours or high for 3 hours. Add the collards, stir, and continue cooking for 2 hours (low) or 1 hour (high).

Serve in large bowls over steamed rice.

Chef's Notes: *Greens can be bothersome to clean, dry and chop, and frozen collards are a second rate substitute for recipes like this one—so look for bags of cleaned, chopped greens at your grocery store or your local farmers' market. Alternatively, have your children, spouse, or in-laws do the washing and chopping.*

WINE SUGGESTION: A nice Sauvignon Blanc from California or perhaps a Sancerre or Pouilly-Fumé from France.

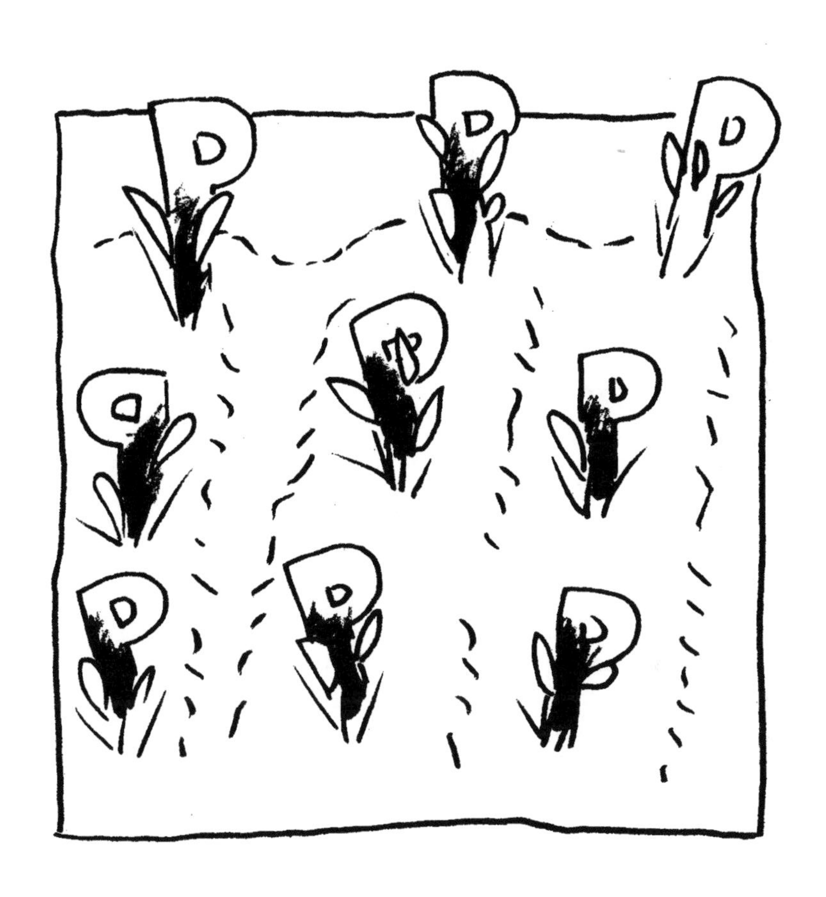

Field Peas

8–10 SIDE SERVINGS

JOE'S MOTHER, WHOSE VEINS CARRIED A BIT OF BLUE BLOOD, never cared for field peas. She thought them too "country" for her citified sensibilities, and found their flavor much too earthy. Unsurprisingly, Joe hardly knew of their existence as a young child.

Then when he was about twelve years old, Joe spent a summer visiting his cousin (on his father's side), Ellie Jo McSimms. Her paw, ole "Kentucky Joe" McSimms, had a farm up in delta country. Ellie Jo was twelve too, and so was her friend Nadine from down the road a piece—although to Joe she seemed a lot older. Nadine's long wavy blonde hair always appeared in need of a brushing, and she wore a length of rope as a belt, even though her blue jeans were plenty tight enough to stay up without one. She took a shine to Joe and gave him a private tour of her family's farm, starting behind the woodshed then going down to the fertile bottomland. She showed him her ripening melons, her little sweet potato patch, and her pumpkin mounds, and then afterwards fed him field peas down by the pond. Joe fell in love with everything "country." Here's Nadine's secret recipe.

2 lbs frozen field peas
½ lb cubed seasoning ham
½ teaspoon salt
½ teaspoon thyme
½ teaspoon crushed red pepper
½ cup chopped celery
3 cups beef broth or stock
1 cup chopped onion

Place all ingredients into the crock, stir to mix, and cook on high for 4 hours or low for 7–8 hours.

WINE SUGGESTION: Boone's Farm Strawberry Hill or any nice muscadine.

HEY, JOE

Creole Cassoulet

SERVES 8–10

THIS RECIPE CAME TO JOE IN A DREAM. Running through a field of sunflowers in the south of France, he was chasing a beautiful young "mademoiselle," always getting closer, yet never quite catching her. He pursued her through Provence, then across the ocean to Louisiana. During the entire course of her flight, she was also cooking cassoulet and shouting out the names of the ingredients in French—first loudly, then softly, as if enticing Joe to "répétez." Somewhere around Grosse Tête, between Lafayette and Baton Rouge, he came so close to mademoiselle that her wind swept hair brushed his face, and the intoxicating scent of simmering flagolets filled his nostrils. He woke up and she was gone, but he quickly wrote down the recipe. This is the translation, with local ingredients substituted as appropriate.

- **1 lb Great Northern Beans**
- **8 skinless chicken thighs and/or drumsticks—about 2½ lbs**
- **1 teaspoon salt**
- **½ teaspoon black pepper**
- **½ teaspoon white pepper**
- **½ teaspoon cayenne pepper**
- **1½ teaspoons thyme, divided**
- **½ lb bacon, cut in 1-inch pieces**
- **2 cups chopped onion**
- **1 cup chopped celery**
- **½ cup chopped bell pepper**
- **8 peeled garlic cloves**
- **2 tablespoons tomato paste**
- **1 bay leaf**
- **2 cups dry white wine**
- **¾ lb Italian sausage, cut into 2-inch pieces**
- **¾ pound pork butt, cut into 1-inch cubes**

Rinse the beans and place them in a non-reactive pot, add water to cover the beans by 2 inches, and let them soak overnight, covered, in the refrigerator. In the morning, place the uncovered pot over a medium heat and bring to a gentle boil. Simmer for about 5 minutes, remove from heat and set aside, covered, while preparing the other ingredients.

Combine the salt, black, white and cayenne peppers, and ½ teaspoon of the thyme. Season the chicken parts with the mixture, rubbing it in with your fingers. Set aside.

In a large skillet set over medium-high heat, cook, and stir the bacon pieces for 2 minutes. Add the onion, celery, bell pepper, and garlic cloves and cook for 5 minutes, stirring occasionally. Stir in the tomato paste, 1 teaspoon thyme, the bay leaf, and wine.

Remove from heat.

Drain the beans and place them in the crock. Stir in the onion-bacon-wine mixture. Place the sausage and pork butt on top of the beans, and the seasoned chicken on top of that. Cover and cook on high for 4½–5½ hours or on low for 9–11 hours.

Chef's Notes: *This dish is great for a large, casual dinner party. Serve with crusty French bread and a simple salad with vinaigrette.*

WINE SUGGESTION: Peut-être un Bourgogne rouge ou un Côtes du Rhône.

Some people say, "Burn, Baby, Burn."
Joe says, "Simmer, Baby, Simmer."

HEY JOE! WHERE YA GOING WITH THAT CROCK IN YOUR HAND?

Veggies and Sides

FROM SOULFUL TO ELEGANT, these side dishes reflect the culinary traditions of France, Africa, and Native America. Several feature variations that can transform them into entrées.

YOODLE OH HO JOE

Collard Greens with Red Bell Peppers

SERVES 6–8

SPRINGTIME IN SCANDINAVIA. Keeping your cool here will be a breeze, thought Joe of his host country's climate. There last April for the annual International Slow Cook Off, Joe felt at the top of his game. Ready to take on his rivals—the borscht belt bred Russian, Vladimir Krokov, and the local champ Bjhrdge the Swede—Joe could taste the sweet ferrous kiss of the Slow Steel Chef first prize trophy.

Presented with a smorgasbord of ingredients with which to create a dish representative of their hometowns, the heat was on for the three finalists. The Russian roasted, the Swede seared, and Joe simmered. Here's his winning entry.

- **1 lb cleaned and trimmed collard greens**
- **2 medium onions, cut in half and sliced into half rounds**
- **4 strips thick sliced bacon, cut into 1-inch pieces**
- **6 ounces cubed seasoning ham**
- **1 red bell pepper, chopped**
- **1 teaspoon salt**
- **½ teaspoon black pepper**
- **¼ teaspoon cayenne pepper**
- **2 cups chicken stock or broth**

Place all ingredients in the slow cooker and stir to mix. Cook on high for 4½ hours.

Chef's Notes: *None. It's perfect as is.*

Smothered Turnip Greens

6 SIDE SERVINGS

- **½ lb mild smoked pork sausage, sliced**
- **1 lb cleaned, chopped turnip greens**
- **2 cups beef broth or stock**
- **1 tablespoon brown sugar**
- **1 teaspoon white wine vinegar**
- **¼ teaspoon hot pepper flakes**
- **1 teaspoon salt**

Combine all ingredients in the slow cooker and stir to mix. Cover and cook on low for 5 hours.

Chef's Notes: *Some grocery stores carry cellophane bags of cleaned, chopped turnip greens in their produce departments. They make slow cooking much easier.*

Corn Macque Choux

SERVES 6–8

"MOCK SHOE"—that's how it's pronounced.

- **1 lb white frozen shoepeg corn**
- **3 ounces salt pork, diced**
- **1 cup chopped celery**
- **3 bay leaves, crushed**
- **½ teaspoon salt**
- **½ teaspoon black pepper**
- **2 cups chopped tomato, fresh or canned**
- **1 teaspoon brown sugar**
- **4 cloves garlic, minced**
- **¼ teaspoon red pepper flakes**
- **1 teaspoon dried basil**
- **2 cups chopped onions**
- **3 tablespoons chopped green onion tops**

Place all ingredients except the green onion tops into the slow cooker and stir to mix. Cook on low for 5 hours. Add the chopped green onion tops and cook an additional 15 minutes.

Chef's Notes: *To prepare as an entrée, add 1½ lbs sliced smoked sausage at the start. Serve over rice if desired.*

WINE SUGGESTION: Whatever you are serving with the entrée, or if this is the entrée, cold beer would be better than wine.

Stewed Okra and Tomatoes

8 SERVINGS

THIS IS A SUMMERTIME FAVORITE AT JOE'S HOUSE. Creole tomatoes and okra are both in season, and fresh is best—but this dish is also delicious using frozen okra and good quality canned diced tomatoes.

- **5 strips thick sliced bacon**
- **3 cups chopped onion**
- **1 tablespoon chopped garlic**
- **1 teaspoon dried basil**
- **1 teaspoon black pepper**
- **1 pinch cayenne pepper**
- **2 lbs sliced okra, fresh or frozen**
- **2 cups diced tomato**
- **1 teaspoon balsamic vinegar**
- **½ teaspoon salt**
- **¼ cup water**

Fry the bacon until crisp and place it on several layers of paper towels to drain. Add the chopped onion to the bacon drippings and sauté over high heat for 6–8 minutes until softened and lightly browned. Add the garlic, basil, black pepper and cayenne pepper and cook for one minute. Remove the pan from heat.

Place the fresh or frozen okra in the crock. Spread the diced tomatoes over the okra and sprinkle on the vinegar and salt. Coarsely chop or crumble the cooked bacon over the okra/tomato mixture. Spread the sautéed onion over all. Use the ¼ cup of water to rinse out the sauté pan, and pour it into the crock. Cook on low for 3–3½ hours. Stir well, adjust seasoning and continue cooking on low for an additional ½ hour.

Chef's Notes: *To prepare as an entrée, add about a pound of either diced ham or sliced smoked sausage, placing it on top of all the other ingredients in the crock. Serve over rice. Makes 5 entrée size servings.*

Here's cookin' with you, Joe.

Creole Succotash

SERVES 8

OKRA REPLACES LIMA BEANS in this lighter and more flavorful succotash.

- **4 tablespoons butter**
- **1½ cups chopped onion**
- **1 cup chopped green bell pepper**
- **1 teaspoon minced garlic**
- **½ teaspoon black pepper**
- **½ teaspoon white pepper**
- **¼ teaspoon cayenne pepper**
- **½ teaspoon salt**
- **2 cups diced fresh tomato, or 1—14½ ounce can**
- **1 lb sliced okra, fresh or frozen**
- **1 lb corn kernels, fresh or frozen**

Melt the butter in a skillet set over a medium heat. Add the chopped onion and bell pepper and sauté, stirring occasionally, for 10 minutes. Stir in the garlic, black pepper, white pepper, cayenne pepper and salt and cook for another minute.

Combine the tomato, okra and corn in the slow cooker. Top with the contents of the skillet, stir to mix, cover and cook on low for 3 hours.

Spinach Rockefeller

SERVES 6–8

ELEGANT, DELICIOUS and very New Orleans in flavor.

- **2 tablespoons butter**
- **1 cup finely chopped onion**
- **1 tablespoon minced garlic**
- **1 tablespoon flour**
- **½ teaspoon white pepper**
- **⅛ teaspoon cayenne pepper**
- **¼ teaspoon nutmeg**
- **1½ cups heavy cream**
- **1 tablespoon Herbsaint or Pernod**
- **½ cup finely chopped green onion**
- **½ cup finely chopped parsley**
- **2 lbs frozen chopped spinach, thawed and drained**

Melt the butter in a skillet set over a medium-high heat. Add the finely chopped onion and sauté, stirring often for about 5 minutes, or until the onions are soft and just begin to brown. Stir in the garlic, flour, white pepper, cayenne pepper and nutmeg and cook 1 minute. Add the cream, and while stirring almost constantly, let the mixture come to a boil. Remove the pan from the heat and stir in the Herbsaint or Pernod and the finely chopped green onion and parsley.

Place the drained spinach in the slow cooker. Add the contents of the pan and mix well. Cover and cook on low for 2 hours.

Chef's Notes: *The best and easiest way to thaw and drain the spinach is in a strainer or colander set over a bowl and left in the refrigerator overnight. When thawed, gently press out any excess moisture.*

Snap Beans in Butter

SERVES 6–8

COOK THIS ONCE, and you will certainly cook it again.

- **1½ lbs snap beans, ends trimmed**
- **¼ teaspoon salt**
- **6 strips thick sliced bacon, cut into 1-inch strips**
- **½ teaspoon black pepper**
- **⅛ teaspoon crushed red pepper**
- **½ cup unsalted butter, melted**
- **1 medium onion, cut into half-circles**

Place all ingredients in the slow cooker and stir to mix. Cook on low for 5 hours.

Chef's Notes: *Substitute 1 lb sliced smoked sausage or andouille for the bacon and serve over rice as an entrée. Makes 4 entrée servings.*

During a recent sojourn in Japan researching his upcoming "Joe Simmer's Asian Slow Cookin'," Joe, for the first time enjoyed haiku, the favorite poetic form of the Japanese. While rummaging through the basement of an old Shinto monastery, Joe unearthed this ancient verse:

So slow is the way
Peaceful kitchen warrior
Cook low until done

—SIMO

GOOOOO JOE!
HELP JOE REBUILD NEW ORLEANS Slowly
Geaux Joe!
VOTE JOE MAYOR!
Green Space!
LIGHT RAIL!
JS

Post-Katrina

SIX MONTHS AFTER HURRICANE KATRINA ravaged New Orleans, Kate Moran wrote in the March 5, 2006 issue of *The Times-Picayune* "The strange cultural crock pot that produced jazz and gumbo came not from suburban subdivisions but from racially mixed neighborhoods of the city". That's when Joe realized this book must be published, and when he decided to include this section of post-K New Orleans recipes.

The hurricane and catastrophic levee failures that flooded 80 percent of the city certainly changed things. Thousands displaced, property destroyed, landmarks lost, death, destruction and despair touching the lives of all New Orleanians. Amidst the ruins that irreverent, insouciant spirit and sense of humor that defines so much of the New Orleans experience still lurks, and sometimes supports the weary population.

Of course we still have to eat, and Joe thought his slow cookin' dishes were recipes for the times—delicious food simmering while freeing you up to fix your roof, gut your house, find a contractor, etc.

Chocolate City Chicken Mole
Category 5 Chili
Mexican Roofer Pinto Beans and Rice
Ninth Ward Smothered Turkey Necks

When Joe evacuated for Hurricane Katrina, he did the "rock star tour," enjoying the hospitality of friends in Houston, Los Angeles, San Francisco, Chicago, Boston, New York, Washington, Atlanta and Miami. To demonstrate his appreciation, he prepared a signature slow cooked dish for every household in which he guested. This year, he's rigged up a slow cooker he can plug into the cigarette lighter in his car, so he can arrive at his hosts' houses, cooked dish in hand.

"Chocolate City" Chicken Mole

SERVES 5–6

GOD, MARTIN LUTHER KING, PANCHO VILLA, and Joe walked into a bar. After a couple of beers and some spirited conversation, they came up with this tasty recipe.

- **3 cups chicken stock (page 119) or broth**
- **3 ancho chiles (dried), stems and seeds removed, torn into pieces**
- **½ cup raisins**
- **¼ cup raw almonds, coarsely chopped**
- **¼ cup raw, hulled sesame seeds**
- **¼ cup raw pumpkin seeds**
- **2 tablespoons butter**
- **2 cups chopped white onion**
- **3 fresh poblano peppers, stems and seeds removed, chopped**
- **1 fresh jalapeño pepper, stems and seeds removed, chopped**
- **1 large fresh tomato, chopped, about 1½ cups**
- **6 cloves garlic, smashed**
- **3 ounces Mexican bitter chocolate, or other bitter-sweet chocolate, broken into small pieces**
- **¼ cup fine, dry breadcrumbs**
- **½ teaspoon ground cinnamon**
- **½ teaspoon ground coriander**
- **¼ teaspoon ground cloves**
- **2 teaspoon salt, or to taste**
- **4½–5 lbs bone-in chicken parts, skinned**

Place the chicken stock in a large blender or food processor along with the ancho chiles and raisins. Blend or process for 20–30 seconds, and allow the chiles and raisins to soak while preparing the other ingredients.

Combine the almonds, sesame seeds, and pumpkin seeds in a dry skillet set over a high heat. Cook and stir for about 5 minutes or until the sesame seeds have browned a bit and the nuts are fragrant, being careful not to let them burn. Transfer to a plate to cool a bit. In the same skillet, melt the butter and sauté the chopped onion, poblano and jalapeño over high heat for about 10 minutes, or until the onion is lightly browned. Remove the pan from the heat and stir in the tomato and garlic.

Pulse the blender or processor containing the stock, chilies and raisins for a few seconds, and then add the toasted nuts and seeds. Blend for about 30 seconds. Add the poblanos, onions, tomato, garlic, chocolate and breadcrumbs and blend until smooth, about 60 seconds. Depending on the size of your blender or food processor, it may be necessary to do this in two batches and then mix them together.

Combine the spices and salt and rub the mixture into the skinless chicken parts. Mix any leftover spice mixture into the sauce. Arrange the chicken pieces in the slow cooker and pour the mole sauce over them. Cover and cook on low for 4–5 hours. Adjust the seasoning and serve with steamed rice.

Chef's Notes: *Jalapeños, poblanos and anchos vary in their "heat" factor. If you want a little more spice, add some cayenne pepper. This dish is better if cooked a day ahead, and reheated on the stove to serve. Leftover sauce can be frozen for later use.*

WINE SUGGESTION: A nice red Rioja or cold cerveza such as Negro Modelo or Bohemia.

Category 5 Chili

SERVES 8

YOU WILL BE BLOWN AWAY by this flood of flavor.

- **1½ lbs ground chuck**
- **1 lb ground chorizo or other hot pork sausage**
- **3 cups chopped onion**
- **5 cloves minced garlic**
- **2½ tablespoons mild chili powder**
- **1 teaspoon cumin**
- **½ teaspoon black pepper**
- **½ teaspoon white pepper**
- **¼ teaspoon cayenne pepper**
- **1 teaspoon oregano**
- **1½ teaspoons paprika**
- **1 teaspoon salt**
- **3 bay leaves, crushed**
- **1½ cups chopped green bell pepper**
- **1½ cups chopped red bell pepper**
- **1 14½ ounce can crushed tomatoes**
- **1 14½ ounce can diced tomatoes**
- **2 15 ounce cans dark red kidney beans**
- **2 cups fresh corn kernels, or 1—10 ounce package frozen corn**
- **½ teaspoon Tabasco sauce, or to taste**
- **12 ounces dark beer**

In a large skillet set over a high heat, cook and stir the ground meats for about 10–15 minutes, or until evenly browned. Using a slotted spoon, transfer the meat to the slow cooker.

Add the chopped onion to the drippings in the pan and sauté, stirring often, for 8 minutes. Stir in the garlic, chili powder, cumin, black pepper, white pepper, cayenne pepper, oregano, paprika, salt and bay leaves and cook for 2 minutes. Transfer the contents of the pan to the crock. Add all remaining ingredients, stir well, cover and cook or high for 4 hours or low for 8 hours.

Chef's Notes: *Pass around bowls of any or all of these suggested toppings to garnish the chili: chopped green onions, chopped fresh or pickled jalapeños, grated cheddar cheese, grated pepper jack cheese, crumbled queso fresco, sour cream, chopped fresh cilantro and tortilla chips.*

WINE SUGGESTION: Beer, of course, or a California Zinfandel or an Australian Cabernet-Zinfandel blend.

JS

Slide behind the wheel of the new HEV-350, JS model and experience the nexus of luxury, performance, convenience and flavor. This 350 horsepower hybrid evcuation vehicle comes factory-equipped with a custom dual power slow cooker. No more fast food or MREs while on the road to somewhere.

Whether your evacuation is mandatory or voluntary, whether you're going with the flow or the contra-flow, you'll be bookin' and cookin' in style.

Mexican Roofer Pinto Beans and Rice

SERVES 6–8

JOE WAS LUCKY. His neighborhood didn't flood, and his house sustained relatively minor wind damage—except for the pecan tree that fell, crushing the back half of his roof. Joe's persuasive way with words, (and a quart of slow–cooked gumbo he had in his new freezer), convinced his insurance adjuster that the whole roof needed replacing. Way to go, Joe! But finding an available roofer in these trying post-K times was another story. So Joe brushed up his Spanish, cooked up a crock of Red Beans and Rice and went to see the crew roofing the house next door. Long story short, they managed to fit in "Casa del Joe" the very next day, and Joe and the crew's boss man, Jose, hit it off like old amigos—drinking, swapping construction work stories and trading recipes. Here's a recipe they came up with together one hot and humid tequila soaked night.

- **1 lb dried pinto beans**
- **6 cups water**
- **3 cups finely chopped onion**
- **1½ cups finely chopped bell pepper**
- **1 tablespoon minced fresh jalapeño**
- **3 bay leaves**
- **2 teaspoons mild chili powder**
- **1 teaspoon ground cumin**
- **1 smoked ham hock, about ¾ lbs**
- **1 teaspoon salt**
- **1 tablespoon vinegar**
- **1 tablespoon olive oil**

Rinse the beans and place them in a large saucepan. Cover with the 6 cups of water, bring the pot to a boil, reduce the heat and simmer for10 minutes. Cover and let soak while preparing the other ingredients.

Place the chopped onion, bell pepper, jalapeño, bay leaves, chili powder and cumin in the crock. Add the soaked beans and stir. Set the smoked ham hock on top and cook on low for 6 hours.

Remove the ham hock and set aside to cool a bit. Remove the bay leaves and discard them. Place ¼ cup of the beans in a small bowl, mash them with the back of a spoon and return them to the crock. Add the salt, vinegar and olive oil. Separate the skin and bone from the cooled ham hock, chop the meat and return it to the crock. Stir, adjust the seasoning, and cook on low for an additional ½ hour. Serve over steamed rice, with additional chopped jalapeño, if desired.

Chef's Notes: *For a real treat, add a few links of Chaurice, or any good hot sausage. One of the good things about this dish is that you can serve it with hot crispy French bread or warm corn tortillas.*

WINE SUGGESTION: A couple of "top shelf" margaritas!

Joe Simmer was one of the first gringos I became friends with after coming to New Orleans. He seemed so international, and made me feel right at home—almost as if he were my brother. We talked about the bean culinary traditions of Mexico and Louisiana, and we came up with this dish. I think you would call it a "fusion dish." It incorporates the flavors and heritage of the old country, with the style and techniques of my new home. And it is quite delicious, if I may say so myself.

—Jose Zima
Roofer

Ninth Ward Smothered Turkey Necks

SERVES 5–6

JOE'S OLD HIGH SCHOOL FRIEND DEWAYNE lived in the "Lower 9th," not far from Fats Domino. Like Fats' big pink compound, Dewayne's place suffered severe flooding after the levee break. Joe put him up for a week or so when he came back to town for some house gutting. He thanked Joe for his hospitality by preparing this delicious dish one night. The Ninth Ward is considered by many to be the soul of New Orleans, and this is some finger licking soul food.

- **3 lbs turkey necks, cut into 3-inch or 4-inch lengths**
- **1 teaspoon salt**
- **1 teaspoon black pepper**
- **½ teaspoon white pepper**
- **¼ teaspoon cayenne pepper**
- **¼ cup olive oil**
- **3 medium onions, cut in half lengthwise and sliced into half-circles**
- **1 large green bell pepper, sliced**
- **8 cloves garlic, smashed**
- **½ teaspoon dried thyme**
- **¼ teaspoon dried sage**
- **2 tablespoons flour**
- **1½ cups chicken stock (page 119) or broth**
- **½ cup white wine**
- **2 tablespoons Worcestershire sauce**
- **1 bay leaf, crushed**
- **¼ cup finely chopped parsley**
- **¼ cup finely chopped green onion**

Rinse the turkey necks and pat dry. Combine the salt and the three peppers and season the necks. Heat the olive oil in a large skillet set over a medium-high heat and quickly brown the turkey necks. Set aside.

Add the sliced onions, bell pepper, and smashed garlic to the pan and sauté 5–10 minutes until the onions are a little browned. Sprinkle in the thyme, sage and flour. Mix well and cook, stirring often, for 3 minutes. Stir in the chicken stock, wine and Worchestershire sauce and mix well, scraping up any bits stuck to the bottom of the pan. Transfer the contents on the pan to the slow cooker. Add the browned turkey necks and the bay leaf. Stir to mix. Cover and cook on high for 3½ hours or low for 7 hours.

Add the finely chopped parsley and green onion, stir and adjust the seasoning. Serve in large, shallow bowls with lots of French bread, or on plates over rice or grits.

WINE SUGGESTION: A Pinot Noir, a full-bodied Chardonnay or perhaps Thunderbird, served very cold.

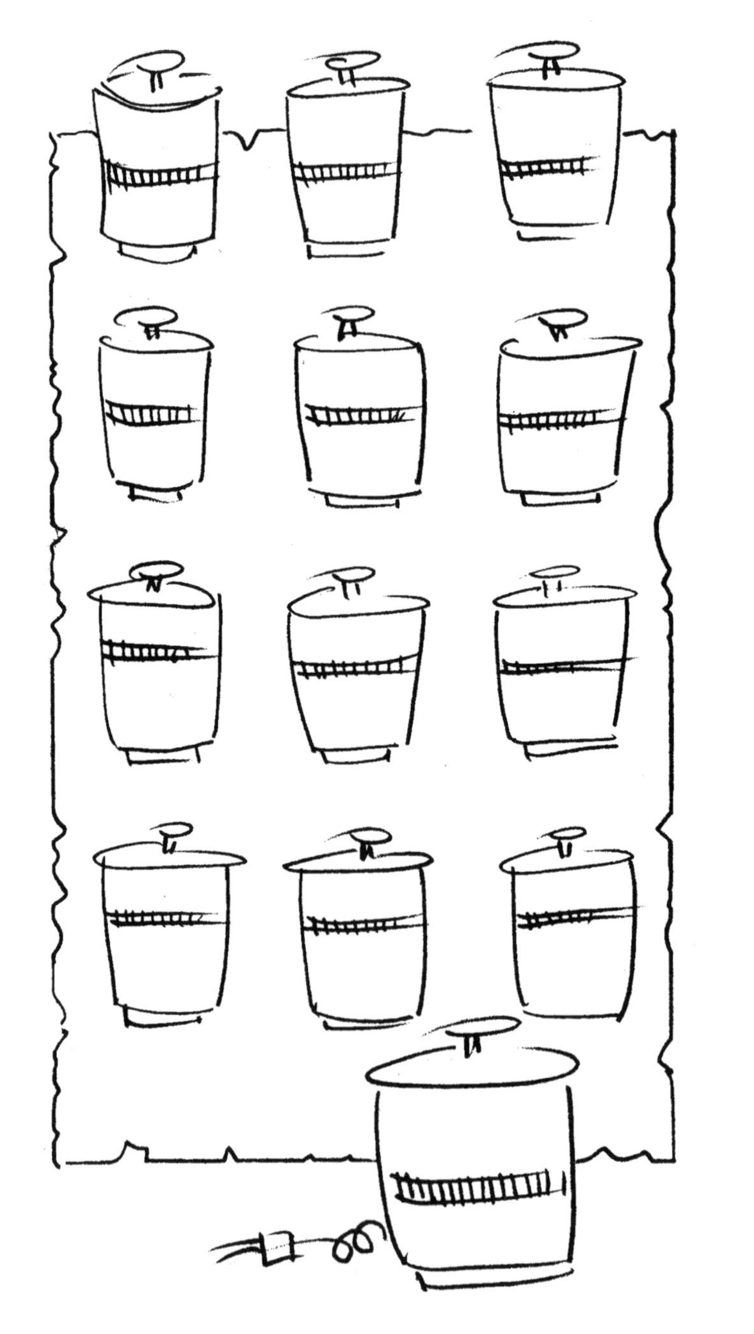

Lagniappe

STOCKS IN A CROCK ARE SO EASY, and well worth the effort. Homemade stock packs a big, flavorful punch, adding depth to so many dishes. The only trick is to make it at least a day ahead so you can let it chill and easily skim away the fat that rises to the top. There's a lot of wiggle room on the cook time for making stock. Just don't cook it less than 5 hours on high or 10 hours on low. Cooking a few hours longer than recommended is fine.

Most stocks will keep in the refrigerator for three or four days, and frozen for six months or more. It is convenient to keep a supply in the freezer packed in a variety of 4, 8, and 16 ounce containers, so you will always have just the right amount handy for any recipe.

Lagniappe, (pronounced lan-yap, for you non-locals) means "something extra," and stock can be something extra if you make it from left-over beef bone, chicken bones, vegetable trimmings, etc. You can store bones and meat scraps in the freezer, then when you accumulate enough, make a big batch of slow-cooked stock. The stock will then give "something extra" to your gumbos, soups, stews, and sauces. May the circle be unbroken.

Rich Chicken Stock

MAKES ABOUT 9–10 CUPS

THIS STOCK IS SO FLAVORFUL, you could dilute it with an equal amount of water and it would still pack more punch than most store-bought varieties.

5 lbs bone-in chicken parts (backs, thighs, drumsticks and/or wings)
1 medium onion, peeled and cut into eighths
1 carrot, scrubbed and trimmed, cut into 1-inch pieces
1 celery stalk, scrubbed and trimmed, cut into 1-inch pieces
1 teaspoon dried thyme
1 bay leaf, crushed
8 cups water

Combine all ingredients in the slow cooker. You may have to adjust the volume of water—add just enough to fill the crock to about one inch from the top. Cover and cook on high for 6 hours or low for 10–12 hours. Strain the finished stock into a bowl or pot, pressing the solids with the back of a spoon to extract as much liquid as possible.

Place the stock in the refrigerator and allow it to chill thoroughly. Remove the solidified fat from the top and discard. The stock can be held refrigerated for 3–4 days, or frozen for 6 months.

Chef's Notes: *For a darker colored, roasted chicken stock, place the chicken parts, onion, carrot and celery on a sheet pan and roast in a 400° oven for about 45 minutes, or until well browned, and then proceed as above.*

Beef Stock

MAKES ABOUT 9–10 CUPS

- **4 lbs sliced beef shanks or other meaty beef bones**
- **1 medium onion, peeled and cut into eighths**
- **1 carrot, scrubbed and trimmed, cut into 1-inch pieces**
- **1 celery stalk, scrubbed and trimmed, cut into 1-inch pieces**
- **1 teaspoon dried thyme**
- **1 bay leaf, crushed**
- **1 clove**
- **8 cups water**

Combine all ingredients except the water on a lightly oiled sheet pan and place in a 450° oven. Roast for 45 minutes to 1 hour. Transfer the browned meat and vegetables to the slow cooker. Pour 1 cup of the water onto the roasting pan and swish it around, scraping up any browned bits, and add to the crock.

Add enough water to fill the crock to about one inch from the top. Cover and cook on high for 8 hours or low for 12–14 hours. Strain the finished stock into a bowl or pot, pressing the solids with the back of a spoon to extract as much liquid as possible.

Place the stock in the refrigerator and allow it to chill thoroughly. Remove the solidified fat from the top and discard. The stock can be held refrigerated for 3–4 days, or frozen for 6 months.

Chef's Notes: *For a stock that is lighter in both color and flavor (and a bit quicker and easier to make), skip roasting the beef and vegetables.*

Roasted Vegetable Stock

MAKES ABOUT 9–10 CUPS

THIS STOCK CAN BE USED IN PLACE OF BEEF STOCK for most pot roast and stew recipes for a lighter, more nuanced flavor.

3 medium onions, peeled and cut into eighths
1 lb mushrooms, cleaned and trimmed
6 carrots, scrubbed and trimmed, cut into 1-inch pieces
1 celery stalk, scrubbed and trimmed, cut into 1-inch pieces
3 small turnips, scrubbed and cut into eighths
12 garlic cloves, peeled and smashed
2 tablespoons olive oil
1 teaspoon dried thyme
3 bay leaves, crushed
3 cloves
Water to cover

Combine the first 6 ingredients on a lightly oiled sheet pan. Add the olive oil and toss to evenly coat the vegetables. Place the pan in a 400° oven and roast for 1 hour and 15 minutes, or until well browned. Transfer browned vegetables to the slow cooker. Pour 1 cup of the water onto the roasting pan and swish it around, scraping up any browned bits, then add it to the crock along with the thyme, bay leaves and cloves.

Add enough water to fill the crock to about one inch from the top. Cover and cook on high for 5 hours or low for 9 to 10 hours. Strain the finished stock into a bowl or pot, pressing the solids with the back of a spoon to extract as much liquid as possible.

Place the stock in the refrigerator and allow it to chill thoroughly. The stock can be held refrigerated for 3–4 days, or frozen for 6 months.

Chef's Notes: *You can skip the roasting stage of this recipe, but the result is a stock with much less depth of flavor, and much lighter in color.*

Seafood Stock

MAKES ABOUT 10–12 CUPS

- **2 lbs small blue crabs, cleaned**
- **1 lb shrimp heads and shells**
- **1 medium onion, peeled and cut onto eighths**
- **1 carrot, scrubbed and trimmed, cut into 1-inch pieces**
- **1 celery stalk, scrubbed and trimmed, cut into 1-inch pieces**
- **3 garlic cloves, peeled and smashed**
- **3 bay leaves, crushed**
- **12 cups water**

Break the legs off of the crabs, and then break the body in half. Place all the parts into the slow cooker, along with all other ingredients. Adjust the amount of water so that the crock in filled to about an inch from the top, cover and cook on high for 5 hours or low for 8–10 hours.

Strain the finished stock into a bowl or pot, pressing the solids with the back of a spoon to extract as much liquid as possible. Chill thoroughly.

Stock can be held in the refrigerator for 3 or 4 days, or frozen for about 6 months.

Chef's Notes: *2 lbs of head-on shrimp will yield about 1 lb of heads and shells. This stock has great flavor and is perfect for a seafood gumbo. It is, however rather murky in color. For a lighter colored, more delicate stock, omit the crabs and use 3 lbs of shrimp heads and shells.*

Joe
JS

WWW.JOESIMMER.COM

Sources

New Orleans Fish House
921 South Dupre Street
New Orleans, LA 70125
800-821-3474
504-821-9700
www.nofh.com
Full line of fresh and frozen fish, shrimp, crawfish, crabmeat, alligator meat, smoked seafood, sausage, andouille and tasso.

Savoie's Sausage and Food Products, Inc
1742 Highway 742
Opelousas, LA
337-942-7241
www.savoiesfoods.com
Pickled pork, tasso, turkey tasso, sausage, andouille.

Uncle Bill's Creole Filé
P. O. Box 169
Baton Rouge, LA 70821
225-267-9220
www.unclebillspices.com
Freshly ground filé.

Louisiana Seafood Exchange
428 Jefferson Highway
New Orleans, LA
800-969-9394
www.louisianaseafood.com
Fresh and frozen seafood, crawfish and shrimp.

Richard's Cajun Foods Corp.
1186 East Ebey St.
Church Point, LA
337-684-6309
www.richardscajunfoods.com
Sausage, andouille, pickled pork and tasso.

WHENEVER TODAY'S FAST PACED WORLD gets Joe's blood boiling, he takes a deep breath, sits down and pulls out the card he keeps in his wallet inscribed with this poem:

"Simmer"
BY JOE SIMMER

Whoa Joe
Let it go, Joe
Just say no, Joe
Simmer

Whoa Joe
Keep it slow, Joe
Let it flow, Joe
Simmer

Whoa Joe
Don't be loco
Find your mojo
Simmer

Whoa Joe
You're a pro, Joe
On HBO, Joe
Simmer

Whoa Joe
Cook it slow Joe
Way to go, Joe
Simmer

Index

D

E

F

Notes to Self

Notes to Joe

Notes to Self

Notes to Joe

Notes to Self

Notes to Joe

Notes to Self

Notes to Joe

Notes to Self

Notes to Joe

Notes to Self

Notes to Joe

HEY JOE
WHERE Y'AT?

Look for upcoming
Joe Simmer titles — some time
in the future

Joe Simmer's
HEALTHY
Slow Cookin'

Joe Simmer's
ALL-AMERICAN
Slow Cookin'

Joe Simmer's
ASIAN
Slow Cookin'

Joe Simmer's
HOLIDAY
Slow Cookin'

Joe Simmer's
ITALIAN
Slow Cookin'

Order copies of
Joe Simmer's CREOLE Slow Cookin'

Internet Order

www.joesimmer.com

Mail Order*

_________ Books at $15.95 each _____________

Shipping $4.00 per book _____________

Tax as applicable** _____________

TOTAL AMOUNT _____________

**9%, Orleans Parish
**4%, other Louisiana residents

*** Please photocopy and send in your order to:***

2 Martini Press, LLC
5500 Prytania Street, #616
New Orleans, LA 70115

BILLING ADDRESS

Name _______________________________________

Address _______________________________________

City/State/Zip _______________________________________

Credit Card ❑ Mastercard ❑ VISA

Acct. No. _______________________ Exp. Date __________

Signature _______________________________________

SHIPPING ADDRESS, IF DIFFERENT

Name _______________________________________

Address _______________________________________

City/State/Zip _______________________________________

2 MARTINI PRESS, LLC
5500 Prytania Street
#616
New Orleans, LA 70115
www.2martinipress.com